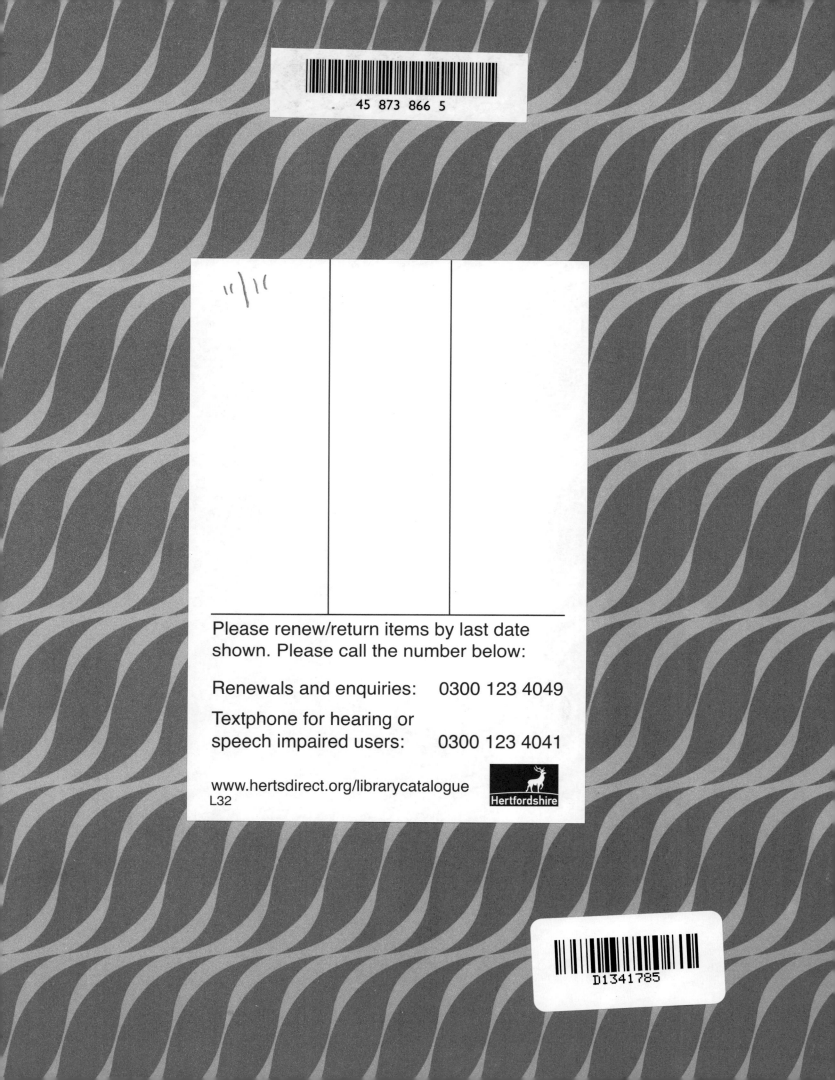

TOUGH & VERSATILE
KNOTS

TOUGH & VERSATILE
KNOTS

*78 key knots made easy in
step-by-step photographs*

GEOFFREY BUDWORTH

southwater

This edition published by Southwater

Distributed in the UK by
The Manning Partnership
251-253 London Road East
Batheaston
Bath BA1 7RL
UK
tel. (0044) 01225 852 727
fax. (0044) 01225 852 852

Distributed in Australia by
Sandstone Publishing
Unit 1, 360 Norton Street
Leichhardt
New South Wales 2040
Australia
tel. (0061) 2 9560 7888
fax. (0061) 2 9560 7488

Distributed in New Zealand by
Five Mile Press NZ
Unit 3/46a Taharoto Road
PO Box 33-1071
Takapuna
Auckland 9
New Zealand
tel. (0064) 9 486 1925
fax. (0064) 9 486 1454

Southwater is an imprint of
Anness Publishing Limited
© 1999, 2000

10 9 8 7 6 5 4 3 2 1

This book is an extract of *The Ultimate
Encyclopedia of Knots & Ropework,* first
published © 1999 Anness Publishing Limited

Publisher: Joanna Lorenz
Project Editor: Helen Marsh
Designer: Michael Morey
Photographer: Rodney Forte
Editorial Reader: Joy Wotton
Production Controller: Julie Hadingham

Printed and bound in Singapore

CAUTION
Do not use any of the knots, bends, hitches, etc., in this book for a purpose that
involves foreseeable risk of loss, damage or injury without the appropriate training and
equipment. Cavers, climbers, rescue workers, wilderness or ocean-going adventurers
who wish to use a particular knot for those (or any other) activities and pursuits are
strongly advised to seek the advice of qualified practitioners first. This book is intended
only to be a safe and simple introduction to knot tying.

Contents

Introduction   6

Basic Knots, Bends & Hitches   28

Bends & Hitches   38

Knots   62

Bindings & Loops   80

Mats, Plaits, Rings, Slings & Things   104

Glossary   124

Index   126

Further Information   128

INTRODUCTION

"It is extraordinary how little the average individual knows about the art of making even the simplest knots."

(R.M. ABRAHAM – *WINTER NIGHTS' ENTERTAINMENTS*, 1932)

Knotting is a great way to occupy one's time. It is a fascinating hobby that is practised by many, from the very young through to the very old. Knotting is widely recognized as an important skill to possess in all manner of different situations. Magicians and escapologists, cavers, climbers, sailers and home-makers alike all use knots as vital tools in their chosen hobbies or professions. There are also many who enjoy knot-tying simply for the pleasure of creating an attractive finished product. They can take advantage of the many different branches of decorative knot-tying: macramé, leather-braiding, whip-making, Chinese decorative knotting, Japanese kumihimo, corn dollies, tassels, tatting and crocheting all provide much scope for the enthusiast. Knots can even be used to save lives in certain situations, and this is why the International Guild of Knot Tyers (IGKT), founded in 1982, is now a recognized educational charity.

There are several thousand individual knots, and their variations are almost infinite in number. Expert knot-tyers add more to the existing numbers every year, inventing new alternatives to safety pins, superglues and other fastenings. Knots are extremely versatile, and experimenting with different tying methods is certainly more absorbing than, say, fastening up a zipper! This book does not attempt to cover all the possibilities outlined above, but the seventy or so knots that are covered will enable those who may already possess rudimentary knotting skills to expand their repertoires. Techniques are given for all kinds of knots, both practical and decorative, and clear instructions take the reader through the different stages of tying these tough and versatile knots.

KEY TO KNOT USER GROUPS

Angling/Fishing

Boating/Sailing

Caving/Climbing

General Purpose

Outdoor Pursuits

History, Origins and Uses

Cave dwellers tied knots. The1960s American knotting writer, Cyrus Lawrence Day, believed that knots pre-dated (perhaps by several millenia) the time when humankind learned to use fire and cultivate the soil, invented the wheel and harnessed the wind. Unfortunately, any tangible evidence for this has long ago decomposed, but the first knotted materials are likely to have been vines, sinews and raw-hide strips from animal carcasses. There are some credible clues from non-perishable artefacts dug up by archaeologists that humans used knots and cordage more than 300,000 years ago. However, there is nothing to indicate what knots were employed before the earliest surviving specimens, less than 10,000 years old – fragments of nets, fishing lines, amulets and clothes – found in prehistoric garbage dumps and with mummified bog bodies. So we know that Neolithic folk tied the overhand knot and half hitch, reef

✦ ABOVE
The artful geometry of rope.

✦ BELOW
Codline and water-resistant coir contrast with darkly tarred and weatherproofed, aromatic hemp hawsers and spun yarn.

Practical and decorative marlinespike seamanship.

the time human history was first recorded, the artful geometry of rope was already established, inherited from a prehistoric time beyond the memories of the oldest and wisest scribes.

KNOT LORE
Knotted cords were used in primitive cultures to keep track of dates, events and genealogies; to recount folk lore and legends; as mnemonic memory cues in prayer or confession, and to record trading transactions and inventories. Both the rosary and the abacus probably evolved from knotted cords. The Incas of ancient Peru made ropes of maguey, derived from the tropical agave plants, that were

♦ BELOW
Old glass fishing floats are protected by a network of meshes.

(square) knot, clove hitch and a running noose – and probably others too. They used them to snare animals, catch fish, tote loads, perhaps as surgical slings – and to strangle the occasional enemy or sacrificial offering. The Late Stone Age lake-dwellers of Switzerland were excellent ropemakers and weavers, who also used the mesh knot (similar to a sheet bend) in their nets, and they would have instantly recognized the cord reticules that secure and protect those glass floats – now found in many waterside cafes – which once supported the gill or drift nets of seagoing fishing fleets. Indeed, by

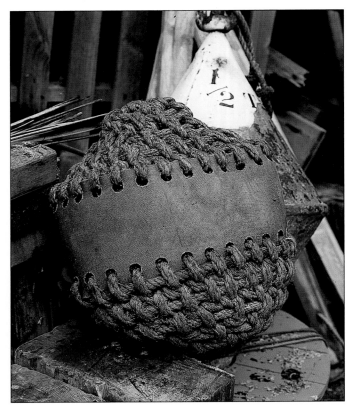

strong enough for the primitive suspension bridges they constructed over mountain chasms. They also produced excellent textiles, and their bureaucracy, lacking a written language, relied upon elaborate coloured and knotted fringes of cord known as *quipus* (Quechua: *quipu* = knot) to keep decimalized records and so administer an empire that extended 4,827 km (3,000 miles) from north to south.

In Hawaii, as recently as 1822, illiterate tax gatherers kept a comprehensive tally of what was collected from each and every inhabitant on the island, in cash or kind, by means of a cord over 800 metres (half a mile) long, to which were attached knots of various colours and materials – one representing dollars, another hogs, others indicating dogs, pieces of sandalwood, and so on.

Ancient Egyptian art tells us regrettably little about their

knots, but we know that they applied the theorem of the Greek mathematician Pythagoras (*c.* 580–500 BC) to solve practical surveying and building problems

by making 12 equal knotted intervals in a rope and then stretching it into a 3,4,5 triangle.

Even the legendary Gordian knot of ancient Greece is a

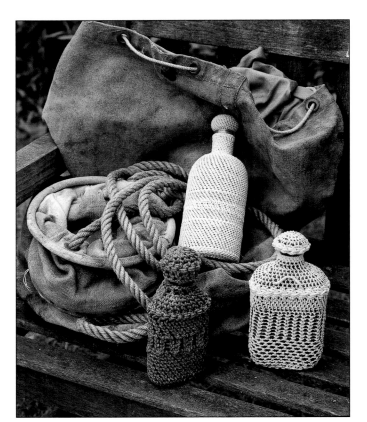

◆ ABOVE LEFT
A "pudding" fender.

◆ ABOVE RIGHT
A boat fender neatly enhanced with a cast-off length of machinery drive-belt in the centre.

◆ LEFT
Needle-hitched bottles or flasks, with a rigger's canvas tool bucket and a kitbag.

◆ OPPOSITE
A sailor's ornate chest becket or handle.

**Whisk brushes, in progress and
completed.**

mystery. Gordius, father of
Midas, was a peasant who rose to
be king of Phrygia and – so the
story goes – tied his by then
redundant farm cart with leather
harness traces and presented it to
the temple of Zeus. So intricate
was the knot that nobody could
untie it, and the oracles
proclaimed that whoever did so
was destined to become emperor
of all Asia. Alexander the Great
tried his hand at this knotted
puzzle but soon lost patience and,
according to one account, severed
it with his sword. "To cut the
Gordian knot" came to mean
disposing of any intractable
problem at a stroke.

SAILORS AND COWBOYS

It is not necessary to like boats to
enjoy knot tying. Indeed boating
these days yields few opportunities
to tie knots. It is equally wrong to
assume that knot tying emerged
only from sailing-ship crews.
It is true that it flourished when

ropework evolved aboard the
massive square-rigged warships
and merchantmen of the 18th and
19th centuries when sailors had
to cope with increasingly complex
rigging. The sailor's chest becket
or handle shows how seamen
then turned in their leisure hours
from practical to ornamental
knotwork. This era lasted,
however, for barely 150 years.
Cowboys tied fancy knots and
braids every bit as elaborate as
those done by sailormen. Ashore,

knots had always been tools for
those who engaged in particular
trades and pursuits: archers and
anglers, basketmakers, bellringers,
bookbinders, builders and
butchers, carters, cobblers and
cowboys, dockers (longshoremen),
falconers, farmers, firemen and
fishermen, gunners, jewellers,
millers, pedlars and poachers,
riggers (in circus and theatre),
shopkeepers, soldiers, steeplejacks,
stevedores and surgeons,
waggoners and weavers. There

◆ BOTTOM
Cargo-handling hooks for dockers (longshoremen) – or prostheses for disabled pirates.

◆ BELOW
A monkey's fist door-stop.

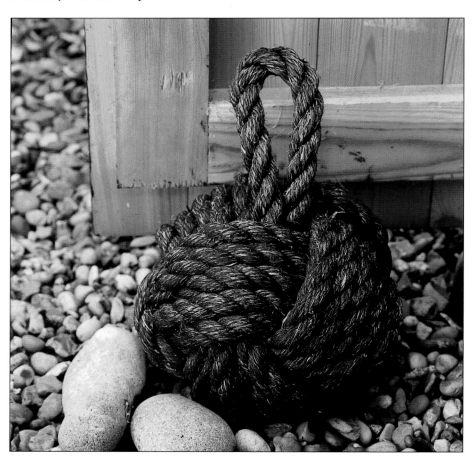

was a time when a handy whisk (brush) and maybe a chunky door-stop, both made from rope, could be found in many homes.

MYSTICS AND MEDICS

The practice of knotting is an ancient one. Knots were believed by some to possess supernatural properties and wizards and witches were known to have traded upon that fact. The legendary Greek epic poet Homer (traditionally a blind minstrel living in the 8th century BC) has Aeolus, king of the winds, give Odysseus a leather bag in which all of the winds are tied up.

The Greek philosopher Plato (*c.* 428–347 BC) detested the blacker aspects of knot magic and wrote, in his *Laws*, that those who preyed upon the gullible by

means of knot sorcery should be put to death. As recently as 1718, the Bordeaux parliament in France sentenced someone to be burnt alive for bewitching an entire family by means of magic knots.

In his *Natural History*, the Roman scientist and historian Pliny the Elder (AD 23–79) advised that wounds bound with a Hercules knot (a reef or square knot) healed more quickly. Indeed, those who learn first aid today still use this knot for slings and bandages but are unaware of the reason why.

Preserved in the medical collections of the 4th century AD Greek physician Oreibasius of

◆ BELOW
Antique hardwood fids, used to help
tuck in the working ends of a knot.

◆ BELOW
Classic boat fenders of coir.

Pergamum are 18 knots,
originally described three
centuries earlier by Heraklas
as surgeons' knots. These are
regrettably not illustrated, but
have been interpreted to include
the overhand knot, reef (square)
knot, the clove hitch, a noose,
a fisherman's loop knot, the jug,
jar or bottle sling, Tom Fool's
knot, a cat's cradle, the true
lover's knot, and – quite
possibly – the constrictor knot.

An early Scandinavian form of
birth control, when a couple
decided they had a large enough
family, was to name the last-born
boy Knut (meaning "knot"). In
some places it was thought that a
cure for warts was to tie knots in
a piece of string, one knot for
each wart, and then to discard the
string; thereafter, the first person
to contact the string would
acquire the warts.

One of the earliest heraldic
knots was the carrick bend used
by the Saxon leader Hereward
the Wake, who in 1071 AD
revolted against William the
Conqueror. In heraldry, it is
still called the Wake knot.

Romantic allusions to the true
lover's knot continually crop up
in English literature after 1495
AD. Although there is no clue as
to whether such a knot existed,
several contemporary knots, with
two interlocking identical parts,
are referred to by that name.

CLASSIC KNOTS
Who invented or discovered all of
these classic knots? Some of the
simpler ones must have arisen
spontaneously, in separate regions
of the world, wherever somebody
picked up a flexible bit of
material and idly toyed with it.
Then again, others are likely to
have been spread by foreign
traders and occupying armies.
Imagine tracing a particular knot
– say the distinctive jug, jar or
bottle sling – from hand to hand
and back through the centuries to
its originator (an impossible
notion, of course). History, as far
as the activity of people was
concerned, might have to be
revised and rewritten.

Materials

Rope has been made by man since the Stone Age, utilising the materials that were available. European hunter-gatherers, 10,000 years ago, grew only one crop – flax – and that was for rope, not food; the ancient Egyptians and Persians made rope from papyrus and flax. Even a captive orang-utan is reported to have made a kind of rope from its bedding material and then swung from it.

It is no surprise that man has gone to such lengths to develop and enhance rope-making materials. Rope enabled humankind to probe the deepest caves and to seek fuel and ores in underground mines; to migrate over rugged terrain with pack animals; to capture, harness and ride other beasts; to sail and cross oceans in search of treasure, trade, conquest and colonization. Rope concentrated the efforts of the labour force that built the great Egyptian pyramids and created the blocks and tackles with which medieval European stone masons erected their Gothic cathedrals and castles.

VEGETABLE FIBRE CORDAGE

As we have seen, until this century, rope was made from the shredded, combed and graded fibres of plant stems such as flax and jute, or from the leaves of sisal and abaca (hemp). It was made from fibres attached to seeds (cotton), and from other vegetable materials as diverse as fibrous coconut shells (coir),

NATURAL ROPE

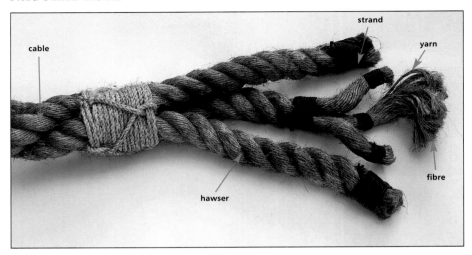

A lefthanded (or S-laid) cable consists of three righthanded (Z-laid) hawsers. Each of these ropes has three lefthanded (counterclockwise) strands made from numerous righthanded (clockwise) yarns, spun from vegetable fibres.

horse and camel (even human) hair, date palms, reeds, esparto grass, wool and silk.

Because of its origins in nature, such cordage is also referred to as natural fibre. These fibres were spun clockwise (or righthanded) to create long yarns. Several of these yarns were next twisted up anticlockwise (counterclockwise) into strands. Finally, three strands were laid up clockwise or righthanded which created a typical rope.

The incurably romantic – who wish that square-rigged sailing ships were still commonplace – regret the demise of these vegetable fibre ropes, with their evocative smells and every shade of gold and brown; but, with the emergence of synthetic (manmade) cordage, the shortcomings of natural fibre ropes became intolerable. They were comparatively weak, even when scaled up to enormous diameters. Unable to withstand

SYNTHETIC (MANMADE) ROPE

A 14 mm (7/12 in) diameter, soft matt polyester, 16-plait sheath encloses a hawser-laid core of several thousand high-tenacity polyester filaments.

◆ BELOW
Vegetable fibre knotted cordage in its natural element.

◆ BELOW
Natural fibre ropes vary in colour and may be blonde or brunette.

much abrasion, vegetable fibre cordage was also prey to mildew, rot, insects and vermin. It swelled when wet (so knots became impossible to untie) and froze in icy conditions with irreparable weakening as brittle fibres broke. Such ropes were also rough on the hands.

Obtainable only from specialized sources, and at a premium price, the use of natural fibre cordage is now very limited, – except in situations (such as filming a costume drama, rigging a classic wooden boat, and designing the interior decor and window dressing of nautical pubs, clubs and restaurants) where the appearance of an earlier period must be evoked. Some thoughtful

souls, however, concerned by what they perceive to be a profligate use of the earth's finite resources, prophesy an eventual return to natural fibre cordage, the raw materials of which can be harvested from renewable growing crops, without destructive ecological footprints.

Sisal rope is still sold for general purposes. Children shin up best-quality soft hemp ropes in school gyms. Coir is used for boat fenders. And for weather-resistant serving and seizing of wire and rope rigging by professional riggers, balls of tarred hemp spun yarn are still sold in several sizes.

It used to be that a rope could only be as long as the ropewalk (open field or long shed) where it

was made – although, of course, two or more could then be spliced together – but compact modern machinery has overcome this and, with extruded synthetic filaments, rope of practically any length can be made.

SYNTHETIC (MANMADE) CORDAGE

Discovered and developed by research chemists in the 1930s, the basic elements for synthetic cordage are: very fine continuous clusters of multifilaments, less than 50 microns/$\frac{1}{500}$ in across and of uniform diameter and circular cross-section; coarser monofilaments, individually more than 50 microns/$\frac{1}{500}$ in in diameter; discontinuous staple fibres (from

Terylene and Dacron); poly-propylene, which is best for mundane domestic use; polyethylene (or Polythene), often sold as balls of twine; and a few so-called "miracle fibres" (such as Kevlar, Dyneema or Spectra) representing the latest and more expensive cutting edge of ropemaking technology. There are two grades of nylon: Nylon 66, discovered in the Du Pont laboratories, was the first manmade fibre of merit available to the cordage industry, and Nylon 6, subsequently developed by I.G. Farbenindustrie. Terylene was a British development from investigations at the Calico Printers Association, the sole rights were then taken up by Imperial Chemical Industries.

2 cm/⅝ in to 2 m/2 yd in length) made by cutting multifilaments or monofilaments into discrete lengths; and flat, narrow, ribbon-like strings produced from extruded split or fibrillated film. The brightly coloured balls of twine often found in hardware shops and stores are usually split film products, as are the larger balls and cops (cylindrical reels) sold at garden centres for horticulture use or as baling twines for agricultural machinery.

All of these raw materials make cordage that is size-for-size stronger and lighter than its vegetable fibre equivalent. A three-strand nylon rope is more than twice as strong as a manila one, yet it weighs half as much and may last four to five times as long. Many can be dyed a variety of colours (even including psychedelic patterns). Almost as strong when wet, they have a high tensile (breaking) strength and are also able to withstand sudden shock loading. Although not

plagued by the ills that afflict natural fibre ropes, they are more susceptible to heat generated by friction – softening, melting and even parting in extreme cases.

The most common manmade materials are: polyamide (nylon), the strongest man-made cordage; polyester (best known trade names

♦ RIGHT
Man-made cordage is smoother than
natural yarn, but stronger.

MANMADE MATERIALS

"MIRACLE FIBRES"

Kevlar – discovered by Du Pont as long ago as 1965 – is an organic polymer immune to moisture and rot. Weight-for-weight it is twice as strong as nylon, but with low elasticity, and it has been used to replace wire halyards. Then there is Spectra or HMPE, the brand name of Allied Chemicals who manufactured this super-lightweight polyethylene (marketed by others as Dyneema and Admiral 2000). Its phenomenal tensile strength is greater than that of stainless steel. Released in 1985, it looks set to supersede Kevlar. The considerable cost of these will not deter ocean yacht racers or climbers, for whom competitive edge and extra safety margins are worth any price, but they are not recommended for routine knot tying.

POLYAMIDE (NYLON)

Polyamide is the strongest manmade cordage (although 10–15 per cent less when wet) and cheaper than polyester. It is very elastic, stretching under a load anything from 10 per cent to 40 per cent, then regaining its original length when the load is removed. This makes it suitable for mooring lines, also towing and rock-climbing ropes – but not in the restricted space of caves or crowded moorings, where stretchy ropes could be a liability. It does not float, so nylon can also be used for yachting anchor warps. The best colour to buy is white, as colouring may weaken the fibres by 10 per cent (while certainly adding a lot to the price). A fairly high melting point of up to 260ºC (478ºF) ensures a reduced risk of melting due to friction; but be warned, it will, like all synthetics, soften and be irredeemably weakened at a much lower temperature than its melting point. Polyamide withstands attack from alkalis (and acids, to a lesser degree), oils and organic solvents. It has acceptable resistance to photochemical degradation from the ultra-violet wavelengths in sunlight, and to abrasion. Domestic consumers of this product will be impressed to learn that it is recommended for deep-sea towing and widely used in the off-shore oil industry.

POLYESTER (TERYLENE, DACRON)

Three-quarters the strength of nylon (but equally strong wet or dry), polyester does not stretch half as much, and pre-stretching during manufacture can remove most of the latent elasticity it does possess. Consequently it is recommended for standing rigging, sheets and halyards, where stretch is unwanted but high tensile strength is required, even replacing wire. It resists acids (and alkalis, to a lesser extent), oils and organic solvents. Like nylon, it does not float and it has about the same melting point and resistance to sunlight – but polyester wears better.

POLYETHYLENE (POLYTHENE)

Cheap, light (but it barely floats in water), without much stretch, polyethylene is fairly hard-wearing and durable but has the lowest melting point of the four "poly" materials. It is sold in hardware stores as balls of twine and is used in the fishing industry, but it is too stiff and springy for most knot tying.

POLYPROPYLENE

In terms of cost and performance, this cordage may be ranked between vegetable fibre and the superior (nylon, terylene) manmade fibre cordage. Made from multifilament, monofilament, staple fibre or split film, it is the most versatile of synthetic fibres. Large quantities are manufactured and sold, at reasonable prices, via hardware and DIY shops and stores for all kinds of mundane work entailing no high performance risks. It has one-third to half the breaking strength of nylon and a much lower melting point – around 150ºC (302ºF) – rendering it useless for any task where friction generates anything approaching that amount of heat, but, as it is the lightest of the synthetics, and floats indefinitely, it is the obvious choice for lifelines and water-skiing towlines. It is completely rot-proof and resistant to most acids, alkalis and oils, but affected adversely by bleaching agents and some industrial solvents, while some cheaper brands denature in bright sun. For lovers of traditional cordage, there is a light brown rope – reliable, hardwearing and inexpensive – made from polypropylene to resemble hemp.

Types of Rope

Vegetable fibres are short and must be spun and twisted to create the long yarns and strands needed for rope. It is the countless fibre ends that give traditional ropes their characteristic hairy appearance and useful surface grip. Long synthetic filaments run the full length of the ropes they form, so manmade cordage is smooth – unless the filaments are purposely chopped into shorter lengths of staple fibres to make ropes that recapture the desirable handling qualities of the older natural cordage. More fibres and yarns make thicker cordage, and a rope that is twice the diameter of another will, as a general rule, be four times as strong (because the cross-sectional area has been quadrupled).

LAID

It is the twist and counter-twist imparted during manufacture that holds rope strands together and gives them their geometry, strength and flexibility. If very little tension is applied during the ropemaking process, the product will be floppy and flexible (soft laid), whereas great tension produces stiff (hard laid) stuff. Hard laid lines wear better but soft laid ones are preferable for tying knots. A three-strand rope is known as a hawser (and so is hawser-laid). Three hawsers laid up lefthanded make a nine-strand cable. Four-strand (shroud-laid) rope is less common and requires a core of yarns to fill the hollow space that inevitably occurs at the heart of such ropes. Lefthanded hawsers (and righthanded cables) are rare but not unknown. Textile workers, weavers and braiders prefer the terms S-laid (lefthanded) and Z-laid (righthanded) for the alternating twist and countertwist of yarns, strands and ropes.

BRAIDED

Braided vegetable fibre cordage has always been rare, except in small sizes for flag halyards and sash window cord. In synthetics it is commonplace and in many ways preferable to strands. An 8- or 16-plait (braid) is more flexible and stretches less than laid line. It does not kink, nor does it impart a spinning motion when loaded (as laid lines tend to do). Some braided cordage is hollow. In most, however, a separate core provides strength, elasticity and other essential properties, reinforced by the sheath, which adds extra surface characteristics, such as friction, feel, resistance to abrasion, sunlight and chemicals. This core may take several different forms, in which a braided outer sheath encloses heart strands that can be braided, laid or composed of parallel multifilaments, monofilaments or yarns. Braid-on-braid is acknowledged to be the strongest of cordage constructions and braided synthetic lines are the most versatile of all cordage.

PLAITED

Eight or sixteen ropes, usually nylon, are woven in pairs to create mighty mooring warps for supertankers.

SHEATH-AND-CORE

Climbing ropes are a special class of cordage, often referred to by the European designation kernmantel (core-sheath). Static ropes take the full weight of climbers and are designed for the wear, tear and occasional short fall of regular climbing; while dynamic ropes are used for safety, generally unloaded, but with the extra elasticity and integral strength to cope with potentially disastrous falls and uncontrolled spins. Single ropes are manufactured in 11 mm/$\frac{2}{5}$ in diameters, plus or minus 5 mm/$\frac{1}{4}$ in, while half-ropes of 9 mm/$\frac{3}{8}$ in diameter, plus or minus 2 mm/$\frac{1}{12}$ in, are intended to be used doubled. Climbing ropes should have high melting points to absorb the heat generated by abseiling (rappelling) and belaying. Obtain specialist advice on the detailed properties of these ropes and look for the UIAA (Union Internationale des Associations d'Alpinisme) label of approval.

Kernmantel accessory cord, used for slings and other attachments, can be obtained in diameters that range from 4–11 mm/$\frac{1}{6}$–$\frac{2}{5}$ in.

Woven nylon webbing comes in widths from 10–75 mm/$\frac{5}{12}$–3 in, but the width most commonly seen is 25 mm/1 in. A tubular tape, resembling a flattened hollow tube, handles and knots easily due to its suppleness, but a flat weave, similar to that found in car seat belts, is stronger, stiffer and has better resistance to wear and abrasion. It is highly versatile and not too expensive for harnesses, belts and slings, and it also makes excellent luggage rack lashings (straps) for cars and vans.

KEY TO TYPES OF ROPE

1   8-strand nylon, 16 mm/$\frac{2}{3}$ in anchor braid.

2   3-strand nylon, 14 mm/$\frac{7}{12}$ in hawser.

3   3-strand polyester, 14 mm/$\frac{7}{12}$ in hawser.

4   3-strand spun polyester, 14 mm/$\frac{7}{12}$ in hawser (resembling natural fibre rope).

5   3-strand monofilament polypropylene, 14 mm/$\frac{7}{12}$ in hawser.

6   3-strand staple/spun polypropylene, 14 mm/$\frac{7}{12}$ in hawser.

7   16-plait matt polyester, 14 mm/$\frac{7}{12}$ in braid-on-braid rope, with an unusual core (itself a 16-plait enclosing an 8-plait), creating three concentric layers.

8   16-plait matt polyester, 16 mm/$\frac{2}{3}$ in braid-on-braid rope (with a double layered core, as above).

9   16-plait pre-stretched polyester, 16 mm/$\frac{2}{3}$ in braid-on-braid (with an 8-plait core) rope.

10 16-plait Dyneema, 12 mm/$\frac{1}{2}$ in braid-on-braid rope (with a two-layered core).

11 16-plait Dyneema, 10 mm/$\frac{5}{12}$ in braid-on-braid rope (with a two-layered core).

12 16-plait polypropylene, 9 mm/$\frac{3}{8}$ in braid-on-braid cord (with a hard-laid 8-plait cord core).

13 16-plait polyester, 6 mm/$\frac{1}{4}$ in sheath-and-core cord (with a heart of four 3-strand strings).

14 8-plait matt polyester, 10 mm/$\frac{5}{12}$ in braid-on-braid rope (with an 8-plait core).

15 8-plait multifilament polypropylene, 8 mm/$\frac{1}{3}$ in braid-on-braid cord (with an 8-plait core).

16 8-plait pre-stretched polyester, 6 mm/$\frac{1}{4}$ in sheath-and-core cord (with a heart of three 3-strand strings).

10   11   12   13   14   15   16

Breaking Strengths

Ropemakers' brochures and leaflets usually contain tables listing the minimum average breaking load of every type and size of their cordage products. Unfortunately, the data differs from company to company, depending upon the tests and equipment each firm uses, making comparisons difficult.

SPECIFICATIONS

Product specifications may blur the facts: for example, a "mooring line", made for specialized markets, may consist of an elastic nylon core inside a hard-wearing polyester sheath, while many mass-produced and comparatively cheap cordage items, sold for the domestic market, can be much weaker. Nevertheless, an appreciation of the main rope and cordage

species can be gained from the following outline. The minimum breaking strength of a 4 mm/$\frac{1}{6}$ in diameter slim nylon cord of 3-strand or 8-plait construction is likely to be around 320 kg/705 lb, which might withstand two 159-kg/25-stone Japanese sumo wrestlers having a tug-of-war. For standard 3-strand polyester of the same diameter the figure is a trifle lower – 295 kg/650 lb – but an 8-plait construction combined with pre-stretch treatment changes that to around 450 kg/990 lb. Polypropylene of the same diameter is variously quoted at 140 kg/309 lb, 250 kg/551 lb and even 430 kg/925 lb; polyethylene is about 185 kg/408 lb, while the average breaking strength of a 4 mm/$\frac{1}{6}$ in cord of Dyneema/Admiral 2000/Spectra is a remarkable 650 kg/1,432 lb. To

achieve these kinds of performance with natural fibres, it would be necessary to have at least a 25 per cent increase in diameter to 5 mm/$\frac{1}{5}$ in manila or 33.3 per cent to 6 mm/$\frac{1}{4}$ in sisal.

LARGER SIZES

With a 10 mm/$\frac{5}{12}$ in thin nylon 3-strand hawser, the minimum breaking strength increases to around 2,400 kg/5,292 lb. That is almost two-and-a-half metric tonnes, the weight of a large motor vehicle. Again, the average figure is somewhat less for polyester at 2,120 kg/about 2 tons; 1,382 kg/1$\frac{1}{3}$ tons for polypropylene; and 1,090 kg/just over a ton for polyethelene. Dyneema/Admiral 2000/Spectra, by contrast, would be about 4,000 kg/about 4 tons. The same size of rope in manila could only cope with 710 kg/1,565 lb and sisal with 635 kg/1,400 lb.

Finally, for a sizeable 24 mm/1 in rope diameter, the average quoted breaking strengths are: nylon = 13 tonnes/12.8 tons; polyester = 10 tonnes/9.8 tons; polypropylene = 8 tonnes/7.9 tons; polyethylene = 6 tonnes/5.9 tons; and Dyneema/Admiral 2000/Spectra = a stupendous 20 tonnes/19.7 tons. Even the best manila would have to be nearly twice that size (and four times as strong) to match those figures.

◆ LEFT
Vegetable fibre cordage is much weaker and generally has a shorter life than synthetic products.

✦ BOTTOM
Synthetic cordage is much stronger and generally has a longer life than products made from vegetable fibre.

COMPARING AND CONTRASTING NATURAL FIBRE AND SYNTHETIC FIBRE ROPES

	·········· NATURAL FIBRES ··········				·········· SYNTHETIC FIBRES ··········			
	Sisal	Cotton	Hemp	Manilla	Polyethylene	Polypropylene	Polyester	Polyamide
Shock loading	●	●	●●●	●●	●	●●●	●●	●●●●
Handling	●	●●●●	●●●	●●	●●●	●●●	●●●●	●●●●
Durability	●	●●	●●●●	●●●	●●	●●●	●●●●	●●●●
Rot & mildew resistance	●	●	●	●	●●●●	●●●●	●●●●	●●●●
U.V. resistance	●●●●	●●●●	●●●●	●●●●	●●	●	●●●●	●●
Acid resistance	●	●	●	●	●●●●	●●●●	●●●●	●●●
Alkali resistance	●●	●●	●●	●●	●●●●	●●●●	●●●●	●●●●
Abrasion resistance	●●	●●	●●●	●●●	●●	●●	●●●●	●●●●
Storage	dry	dry	dry	dry	wet or dry	wet or dry	wet or dry	wet or dry
Buoyancy	sinks	sinks	sinks	sinks	floats (just)	floats	sinks	sinks
Melting point*	not affected	not affected	not affected	not affected	about 128°C (about 262°F)	about 150°C (about 302°F)	about 245°C (about 473°F)	about 250°C (about 482°F)

Key: ● poor ●● acceptable ●●● good ●●●● excellent
* Note that cordage softens and weakens at perhaps 20–30 per cent lower temperatures.

SUMMARY

These data take no account of fair wear and tear (including knots), damage or misuse (e.g. shock loading, or excessive friction). Consequently a safe working load will be considerably less – perhaps a fifth to a seventh of the quoted strengths. Then again, it is often necessary to buy synthetic cordage many times stronger than actually required; for example, a 4 mm/⅙ in cord would not match a block and tackle made for 25 mm/1 in rope even though it might be able to cope with the intended load, nor could it be comfortably grasped in the hand and heaved.

Knot tyers do not normally need to know either the molecular structure of cordage or its test data interpreted in charts and graphs. Cavers and climbers, flyers (of gliders and microlight aircraft), and all who calculatingly engage in potentially hazardous pursuits – from astronautics to undersea exploration – can obtain these technical details from the manufacturers. For the average user, a general knowledge of the main types of cordage is all that is needed to buy shrewdly and sensibly.

Care of Cordage

Do not leave rope or smaller stuff (cotton, thread or string) exposed needlessly to bright sunlight. Avoid any chemical contamination (for example, car battery acid). Protect synthetics from heat-generating friction, spark-spitting camp-fires or acetylene-cutting torches, and all other kinds of combustion. Try to avoid letting wet rope freeze. Store cordage in a dark, dry and cool place with good air circulation; relative humidity should be 40–60 per cent and the temperature10–20°C (50–70°F). Wash dirty ropes in warm water to remove abrasive grit from their fibres and then dry them gently; similarly, at the end of a sailing season, soak and rinse in fresh water ropes that have been exposed to salt crystals. Abrasion can result from careless

♦ ABOVE
WRAPPED & REEF KNOTTED COIL
Rope and smaller cordage alike may be transported this way, in a bag or the boot (trunk) of a motor vehicle, with a realistic hope that it may be retrieved tangle-free at the end of the journey.

♦ LEFT
ALPINE COIL
Climbers favour this means of carrying their ropes.

handling in a rough environment or from ill-fitting blocks, cleats, or fairleads, but fair wear and tear is inevitable, whether it is from regular use or from being kept in the same position for prolonged periods. Even unused rope that has been carefully stored will age and become less reliable.

INSPECTING ROPES
Inspect ropes periodically, metre by metre/yard by yard in a good light, for loose, worn and broken surface yarns and cut strands. Some surface fluffing is inevitable; it is fairly harmless and might actually afford slight protection from further wear. Chemical attack can show as staining and

◆ BELOW
FIGURE-OF-EIGHT COIL
Storekeepers prefer this method, which
provides a loop for hanging ropes.

◆ BELOW
FIREMAN'S COIL
Elegantly simple, this method deserves to
be better known.

used with lifting tackle must be pensioned off long before they reach such senescence. Each rope should have its own log book in which its working history is recorded. Communal club ropes (that anyone might use at any time) should be retired after two or three years, but individually owned and maintained ropes may be used for four to five years, then down-graded for teaching knots and other points of general use that do not involve climbing.

It has been observed that rope with a mind of its own, awkward to manipulate and a trifle disobedient, is generally at the height of its powers. By contrast, rope that is soft and amenable, a pleasure to handle, should be condemned and discarded. There is some truth in this. Do not tread on rope, allow it to be nipped or become kinked, or drop it from a height. Coil ropes loosely and then hang them up on pegs well above the floor.

softening. Heat damage is harder to identify, unless fusing and glazing are detectable. Internal wear and damage can be seen by carefully opening laid strands but may be concealed in braided stuff (when the core could be weakened while the sheath remains relatively unworn and lacks obvious damage).

So a risk assessment for braided lines must also take into account their recent history of use and abuse. Worn-out rope looks its age. It is often attenuated (weakened by stretching), with a reduced diameter and a more acute angle of lay between the strands. Sheath-and-core ropes can develop creep, the sheath moving separately from the heart strands. Climbing ropes and those

Tools

◆ BELOW
Tying elaborate knots is made easier
with one or more handy tools (see key
to illustration).

Acquire a sharp and robust craft knife to cut rope and cord; scissors work only on thin strings and twines. Most of the knots in this book can be tied and tightened with just the fingers, aided now and then with a prod from the pointed cap of a ballpoint pen. A few (such as the Turk's heads) are more easily completed with one or more of the following tools.

GRIPFIDS
Handmade by rope craftsman Stuart Grainger, these resemble small Swedish fids, with the refinement that the tip clings to working strands, pulling them through knotwork as the tool is withdrawn. Two sizes cope with cordage up to either 7 mm/³⁄₁₀ in or 12 mm/½ in diameter.

NETTING NEEDLES
These serve as bobbins for storing quantities of small cords tangle-free and ready for immediate use. Sizes range from a tiny 11.5 cm/4½ in to jumbo-sized ones 30 cm/12 in or more in length. Shun crudely made ones in favour of those that are polished to a smooth finish. The seller will show you how to load them.

ROUND-BILLED PLIERS
Handy for tightening knots with lots of crossing points. Most high street hardware shops or do-it-yourself superstores will have them. Choose a pair to suit the scale of work: a small size (sometimes called "jeweller's pliers") will have an overall length of about 10 cm/4 in, with more robust sizes from about 15 cm/6 in upwards.

SWEDISH FIDS*
These are used to poke and prize open gaps through which working strands can be tucked and pulled. Obtainable from yacht chandlers and serious rope stockists, they range in length from about 15 cm/6 in to 38 cm/15 in or more. Choose a size to match the scale of your work.

WIRE LOOPS
Homemade from stiff and springy wire 0.25 cm/¹⁄₁₀ in diameter – or thinner – inserted securely into a handle, these are indispensable alternatives to fids when working with smaller stuff.

KEY TO TOOLS	
1	Netting needle (large)
2	Netting needle (medium)
3	Netting needle (small)
4	Gripfid (large)
5	Gripfid (small)
6	Hollow "Swedish" fid (small)
7	Hollow "Swedish" fid (large)
8	Homemade wire loop (large)
9	Homemade wire loop (small)
10	Homemade wire loop (medium)
11	Jeweller's pliers
12	Round-billed pliers

* Originally fids were solid hardwood spikes. They can occasionally be found in antique shops or markets as collectable treen (lathe-turned wood).

Cutting & Securing Ends

TYING & TAPING

Before cutting any natural fibre cordage, first tape or tie it to prevent fraying. Adhesive tape is the least attractive option – and unacceptable on finished craftwork – but it is used a lot in preparatory stages as an easy alternative to whipping. Wrap where the cut is to be made and then simply slice the tape in half to achieve two bound ends at a stroke. Alternatively, tie a pair of strangle or constrictor knots, one on either side of where the cut is to be made.

HEATING & SEALING

This is now widely practised by ropeworkers and riggers. There is no need to tape or tie heat-sealed ends. Rope manufacturers and stockists have electrically heated guillotines to cut-and-seal the ropes and cords they sell. These cost too much for most of us, so the comparatively cool yellow flame of a struck match may have to do on small stuff. For large diameters, or to cut-and-seal a batch of strands, heat the blade of an old penknife in the blue flame of a blow-torch until the tip and edge glow cherry-red. Pause to re-heat it every few seconds for a clean and fast cut. Nylon melts, drips and burns with whitish smoke and a smell said to resemble fish or celery; it may even flash into a small flame (easily blown out). Polyester melts, drips and burns with dense black smoke and a smell like mushrooms. Polypropylene and

TYING

1 Tie two strangle knots, one either side of where the cut will be made.

TAPING

1 Wrap a turn or two of adhesive tape around the rope or cord.

HEAT SEALING 1

With an electric guillotine or a heated knife blade (not shown), cordage and small diameter ropes may be neatly cut and sealed.

polyethylene react at lower temperatures, shrinking rapidly away from the source of heat. It is possible to pinch the soft heated ends to a point, rolling them between forefinger and thumb, before they harden, but take care

2 Slice vertically down halfway between the two binding knots already tied.

2 Cut vertically down through the middle of the taped portion.

HEAT SEALING 2

Use the naked flame of a match or cigarette lighter for a quick but often lumpy seal.

to wet the fingertips first or it may cause a burn and blister. A cord that appears to be synthetic but actually chars and even ignites without melting, is probably made from rayon, which comes from wood pulp.

Terms & Techniques

Anyone who ties a knot is described in knotting circles as a tyer (not tier) since the former is unambiguous while the latter has a different meaning when written.

SIMPLE TERMS

The end actively involved in the tying process is referred to as the **working end** or sometimes – by anglers – as the **tag end**; the in-active remainder is known as the **standing part** and **standing end**. Doubling a line so that two parts are brought close together creates a **bight**. If this is done to locate the exact centre of the bit of stuff in hand, then one is said to **middle** it. Once the two adjacent parts cross, a bight turns into a loop; a further twist creates a couple of **elbows**, while the process of turning a bight or loop into an improvised eye by wrapping the end several times around the standing part is referred to as **dogging**. Any loop that is pulled

---

---

so small that it deforms and damages a rope becomes a **kink**.

The word **rope** is generally defined as meaning any plaited, braided or laid (in strands) product over 10 mm ($\frac{5}{12}$ in) in diameter, although there are exceptions (for example, some

---

climbing ropes are 9 mm/⅜ in diameter). Anything much smaller is referred to as **cord, string, twine** or **thread**. Rope and cord are collectively called **cordage** but, more commonly, **stuff**. A rope or cord dedicated to a particular job becomes a **line** (tow line, washing line, lifeline, throwing or heaving line), or acquires an even more specific label (lanyard, lashing or lassoo). A lightweight throwing or heaving line that is used to haul a heavier line across an intervening space is known as a **messenger**. The terms **plait** and **braid** are virtually interchangeable. There are, however, some who say that braids are flat while plaits have a three-dimensional cross-section.

Ropeworkers often "take a **turn**" in order to check a load by means of the friction it applies. Wrapping the working end an extra amount to bring it alongside the standing part, so as to tie it off, produces a **round turn**. Converting a single-ply knot to two, three (or more) ply involves following the original **lead** of the knot around with the working end. The place within a knot where the collective friction of its parts is concentrated is known as the **nip**. The tuck that finally secures a knot, preventing it from collapsing or unravelling, is the **locking tuck**. A simple loop is an **overhand loop** when the working end lies on top of the standing part, becoming an **underhand loop** if the working end goes beneath the standing part.

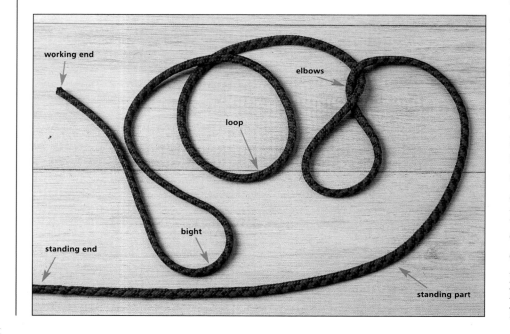

working end

elbows

loop

bight

standing end

standing part

1 More often than not, a clove hitch may have been tied with the working end.

2 But slide the knot sideways off its foundation – and it will fall apart.

3 Once separated from its foundation, nothing remains of the knot but the line in which it was tied.

4 To re-tie the clove hitch, this time in the bight, first cast an overhand loop.

5 Create a second underhand loop immediately alongside the first one.

6 Twist the loops to overlap them. The resulting clove hitch may be slid back on to its foundation.

TYING TECHNIQUES

Most knots can be tied in more than one way. The methods illustrated have been chosen either because they are easier to learn or to photograph clearly. Practised knot tyers develop more dextrous ways to tie knots that are almost sleight of hand. Discover these slicker and quicker tying tricks for yourself: with a completed knot in your hands, back-track, untying the knot a step at a time, to see how it is created. A short cut may occur to you. Re-tie it that way in future.

Tying a knot "in the bight" means doing so without using the working end. When a hitch or a binding knot collapses to nothing if slid from the foundation around which it was tied or a loop knot can be unravelled without recourse to its ends (in other words, it "unties in the bight"), then it can be tied in the bight. This is the "law of hitch & bight" proposed by Harry Asher in the mid-1980s. A surprising number of knots may be tied this way. Knowing the principle can also enable knot tyers to spot subtle differences in seemingly identical knots, and the two knots can be put to their best use on different occasions.

Most knots must be drawn up gradually so as to remove slack and daylight before gently pulling on each end and standing part in turn to create a knot that remains snug and firm.

BASIC KNOTS, BENDS & HITCHES

"Every knot is an exercise in friction ... extreme simplicity can only be had at the expense of effectiveness."

(BRION TOSS –
THE RIGGER'S APPRENTICE, 1984)

All knotting may be summed up under three main headings: Knots, Bends and Hitches. A hitch attaches a line to a post, rail, spar, ring or even another rope; a bend joins two ropes together; a knot is anything other than a bend or a hitch (including stopper knots, binding knots and loop knots) although the word "knot" is also used, sometimes confusingly, in a general way to refer even to bends and hitches. Discover how easily you can tie these basic knots. All you will need is two lengths of flexible cord, each 1–2 m/3–6½ ft long and from 5–10 mm/ ⅕–⁵⁄₁₂ in in diameter.

Most cordage will fray unless the ends are securely treated in some way. A better-looking treatment than taping, tying and heat sealing is a whipping of some kind, and a whipped end is detailed in this section.

Simple, Overhand or Thumb Knot

This is the most elementary stopper knot, to prevent small stuff (cotton, thread or string) from fraying or pulling out of a hole through which it has been threaded. Its uses range from securing thread in a needle to tying loose change into the corner of a handkerchief when on the beach or anywhere else where deep pockets are temporarily not available. Nobody ever has to be taught to tie this knot. It just comes naturally.

1 Make an overhand loop in the small stuff that is to be tied.

2 Tuck the working end through the loop already formed and pull on the standing end to tighten the knot.

Overhand Knot with Drawloop

Drawloops act as quick releases, and may also strengthen some knots by bulking them up with an extra knot part. Overlooked and underrated by many knot tyers, drawloops deserve to be used more, and will from time to time be recommended in this book.

Start to tie a simple overhand knot but stop before the working end has been fully pulled through.

Two Strand Overhand Knot

This is another knot that the youngest person can tie instinctively. It creates a bigger stopper knot, for cottons or domestic string, and also acts to hold cords together as long as they lie in the same direction, for example, to prevent a waist tie in pyjamas, swimming trunks or tracksuit trousers (sweatpants) from pulling out when not in use. NB: This is not a bend because the two cords are not aligned to be pulled in opposite directions.

1 Place the two strings or cords to be tied parallel and together.

2 Tie a simple overhand knot. Tighten, taking care to keep the lines parallel (like railway tracks) throughout.

Double Overhand Knot

This forms a chunkier stopper knot than the simple overhand knot, although it will not block a larger hole. It is, however, an indispensable technique for other knots that are based upon it.

1 Tie an overhand knot – but tuck the working end a second time.

2 Gently pull both ends apart, at the same time twisting them in opposite directions. In the example shown, the lefthand thumb goes up and away from the tyer, the righthand thumb down and away. The cord dictates what it wants to do; simply go along with it. See how a diagonal knot part wraps itself around – let it happen. Pull on both ends at the same time to tighten this knot.

Triple (and Multiple) Overhand Knots

Three (or more) initial tucks produce triple or multiple overhand knots. These can make shortenings and embellishments, such as those seen in the ropes around the waists of nuns and monks, who used this triple knot as a symbolic reference to their threefold sacred vows.

2 Pull both ends, rotating them in different directions so that a diagonal wrapping turn appears.

1 Tie a double overhand knot, then tuck the working end a third time.

3 Shape the emerging knot to bed all of the knot parts down snugly. Tighten by pulling both ends apart.

Strangle Knot

A double overhand knot, tied around something, makes a strangle knot. Use it to seize cut ends of cordage and prevent them from fraying; to secure rolls of anything from carpets to technical drawings and wallpaper, or to clamp do-it-yourself and hobbyists' bits-and-pieces together while the glue hardens. Several other useful binding knots are featured in this book; but, for a start, this one is as good as any. Try it also with a drawloop.

1 Produce a double overhand knot but at this stage keep it very loose.

2 Insert whatever is to be bound, ensure the overriding diagonal lies between the other two knot parts, and tighten the knot by pulling on both ends. The ends can then be cut off short.

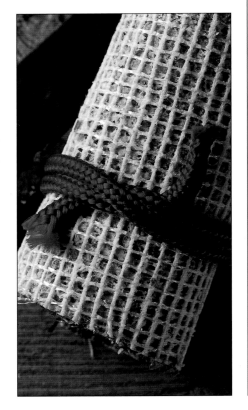

Surgeon's Loop

This is a triple overhand loop, stronger for the extra tuck, and is recommended for angling lines.

Make this knot in dispensable stuff as it is easier to cut it off than to untie it.

1 Make a fairly long bight and tie a treble overhand knot in it.

2 Eliminate any unevenness and mould it with your fingers into a smooth barrel-shaped knot. Anglers may spit on monofilaments to lubricate them.

Double Overhand Loop

This loop is bulkier and slightly stronger than the previous one.

Do not attempt to untie it – cut it off after use.

1 With a somewhat longer bight, tie a double overhand knot.

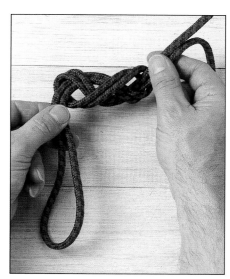

2 Uncross any twisted knot parts and remove any slack until the knot assumes its characteristic shape. Then tighten gradually, pulling on each of the four knot parts in turn.

Strength & Security

Knots weaken the rope, cord or string in which they are tied. An unwanted overhand knot allowed to remain in a fishing line or washing line, for instance, will more than halve the breaking strength. Bulky knots are better, the double fisherman's or grinner knot preserving 65 to 70 per cent of the cordage strength and the blood knot 85 to 90 per cent; while the bimini twist is claimed by some to be 100 per cent efficient (in other words, as strong as the unknotted line). Climbers, whose lives literally hang upon their knots, anglers, keen to preserve expensive tackle and to catch that record-breaking fish, ropeworking assault, rescue or survey teams, lifting tackle operatives on construction sites – all choose and use strong knots.

Security is a different consideration. A strong knot that slips and slides, spills, capsizes or otherwise comes undone, is less secure than one that holds firm. Some knots are secure enough when carefully assembled and placed under a steady load but loosen and come adrift if intermittently jerked or repeatedly shaken.

Since strength and security are different characteristics, knots that combine both of them would seem to be ideal – why bother with any others? This is because ease of tying and untying are often essential. Simplicity too may be desirable. So, when they can get away with it, knot tyers knowingly trade off one quality

Figure of eight loop made even more secure by means of a double overhand knot.

Relatively weak reef knot rendered secure with a couple of double overhand knots.

Climber's strop strengthened and secured with a double fisherman's knot plus taped ends.

against the other. Indeed some classic knots, despite long established reputations for reliability, are surprisingly weak and insecure when put to the test. The common bowline is barely 45 per cent strong and in stiff or slick rope can easily be made to spill.

◆ ABOVE
Strengthened bowline secured with an overhand knot.

Knots can be made more secure. For example, the relatively strong figure of eight loop may be made more secure by attaching the short end of the rope to its adjacent standing part with a double overhand knot (above left). Similarly, the common bowline may be both strengthened and made more secure with the extra turn of this double (or climber's) version, the working end of which is further safeguarded with an overhand knot to the nearest leg of the loop (left). The reef knot is essentially weak, but the two ends may be secured with a couple of double overhand knots (above centre). And a proprietary brand of chock (above right), known as a "wallnut" and used for mountaineering and related activities, is attached to a strop of outstandingly strong "miracle fibre" Spectra accessory cord, which is tied with a double fisherman's knot and security assured by taping both ends to adjacent standing parts.

Double Fisherman's Knot

The strong double fisherman's knot is known to anglers as a grinner knot (presumably because of the gaping mouth formed before the knots slide shut). It is a reasonably secure knot.

1 Place the two lines parallel and close together, tying a double overhand knot with one working end around the other standing part.

2 Turn the half-completed knot end-for-end and tie a second double overhand knot with the other end. Tighten individual knots before pulling on the standing parts to close the knot.

Triple Fisherman's Knot

A triple fisherman's knot is an angler's double grinner knot and is used for thinner, springier or more slippery lines.

Proceed as for a double fisherman's knot – but use triple overhand knots – and tighten similarly.

Perfected Whipping

This treatment for a rope's end is comparatively quick to apply, but is also likely to come untied.

1 Lay both ends of the whipping twine together, pointing in opposite directions, on the rope.

2 Begin to wrap with that part of the twine furthest from the rope's end.

3 Continue to wrap as tightly and neatly as possible, keeping the two underlying twine parts parallel and together, and untangling the working bight (each completed revolution) from the rope's end.

4 As the working bight shrinks, remove the twist that is inevitably imparted to it (better still, with practice, at the start insert a counter-twist that will unwind as the work progresses).

5 Pull on the end of the twine to remove all slack from the final wrapping turn, before pulling steadily on both ends to secure and finish off the whipping.

Scaffold Knot

This is a strong, secure sliding loop. Use it when an eye must be protected from chafe by means of a metal or plastic liner (called a "thimble"). Tighten the loop to grip and hold this particular bit of hardware. With practised fingers, this knot can be tied in no more than 30 seconds and the beauty of it is that the more the strain that's put on it, the tighter this knot will grip.

1 Make a bight and tie a double overhand knot with the working end around the standing part of the line.

2 Pull the end and the appropriate leg of the loop in opposite directions to tighten the knot.

Multiple Scaffold Knot

A triple overhand knot will make a double scaffold knot, which is perhaps slightly stronger. A multiple knot results from a multiple overhand knot, but there is probably little benefit from doing this other than to produce a handsomely handy bulk.

1 Tie a straight forward triple overhand knot in the working end around the standing part.

2 Pull the end and the appropriate loop leg in opposite directions to tighten the knot.

BENDS &
HITCHES

*"To bend two Cabells or Roapes together . . .
when we meane to take them a-sunder againe."*
(Sir Henry Manwayring –
The Sea-man's Dictionary, 1644)

A bend is any knot that joins two ropes or
other lines together. As a general rule, it should
be quite possible to untie bends after use, for
rope is a costly item that may be re-used later
for another purpose. Restrict untieable knots to
string, anglers' monofilaments and other less
expensive stuff, from which they can be cut off
and discarded when no longer needed. Most
bends are made in two separate ends of
identical material.

A line is said to be "made fast" (not "hitched")
to various objects, even another rope, and only
the knot itself is called a hitch. Some hitches
work best with a direct pull at right angles to
the point of attachment; others will withstand
a sideways or varying direction of pull.

Blood Knot with Inward Coil

This is one of the several classic angling knots that, because of their numerous compact wrapping turns, are collectively known as blood or barrel-shaped knots. Numerous wrapping turns make this knot both strong and secure. It is primarily used by anglers, who tie it in their fine lines, but it can prove equally useful, tied in thicker cordage, out of water.

1 Bring two lines, facing in opposite directions, close together, and lay them parallel.

2 With one of the working ends, begin to apply wrapping turns.

3 The first wrap should go around the front and then down the back of both lines.

4 Ensure that the first wrapping turn encloses both of the lines to be joined so as to trap its own standing part.

5 Try to make each wrapping turn lie snugly and tightly beside the previous one.

6 Complete five or six turns, then tuck and trap the working end between both lines.

7 With the other working end, begin the wrapping process again.

8 Repeat the previous steps, wrapping in towards the middle of the emerging knot.

9 Finally tuck the second working end down through the centre of the knot (in the opposite direction to the other end). Mould all of the turns tight, from the outside in, and then pull on the two ends to remove any slack.

Racking Bend

Racking is the term for figure-of-eight interweaving, such as in this instance, where a small diameter messenger line seizes the bight of a much thicker rope. The purpose is to seize and grip the larger rope so that its bight remains closed and does not spring apart. Generally used for heavy-duty appplications, it is however a versatile method, and scale is a relative thing. It can be used to join massive cable-laid cordage aboard ocean-going ships but it could also be applied in fine twines to a model galleon made from matchsticks.

1 Make a bight in the larger of the two lines to be temporarily linked and bring the smaller one over it.

2 Divert the working end to one side, tucking it under one leg of the bight.

3 Bring the working end back across to the other side, going over, then tucking under the bight.

4 Take the working end back across the bight, going over, then feed it back under again.

5 Continue this racking process as far along the neck of the bight as necessary to keep it together.

6 Finally, tuck the working end beneath one of the racking turns as shown. The completed knot must be tightened a turn at a time towards the end of the bight.

Seizing Bend

This is a strong, secure bend that is both quick and simple to tie and remarkably easy to untie. A comparative newcomer on the knotting scene, it was devised and publicized by Harry Asher in 1986.

1 Make a bight in the larger of the two lines to be temporarily joined and tuck the end of the lighter line up through it.

2 Take a turn with the working end of the line around the end of the bight.

3 Divert the working end to one side of the bight and begin to wrap it.

4 Ensure that the first turn traps its preceding standing part.

5 Wrap neatly and snugly towards the end of the bight.

6 Now loosen the initial turn and draw out a loop from it.

7 Pass the loop over the inert end of the bight and pull it tight, so that it holds all of the wrapping turns and traps the working end of the knot. For real security, leave a longer end than shown in the lighter line and fasten it to its own standing part with a bowline.

Albright Special

This tried-and-tested knot is used by numerous anglers to join monofilament to braid, or braid to wire. It is shown here using much thicker cordage than would normally be used. Its first appearance in print was in 1975, but later publications sometimes refer to it as the Allbright Special, so there is some uncertainty as to the correct spelling of the originator's name.

1 Make a bight in the larger of the two lines to be joined.

2 Bring the second line over and parallel with the initial bight.

3 Divert the working end to one side (in this instance the righthand), preparatory to making wrapping turns. Begin the wrapping turns by taking the working end over one side of the bight and back beneath both bight legs.

4 Take the working end back over the top of the bight, trapping its preceding standing part in the process.

5 Continue to wrap over and down beneath the bight legs again.

6 Take a second full wrapping turn neatly alongside the first one.

7 Complete as many turns as necessary for a secure and stable knot.

8 Finally, tuck the working end down through the original bight.

Simple Simon Over

This knot (and two variations of it) were devised by Harry Asher and published in 1989. It is especially effective in slick synthetic lines and, once mastered, it can be tied easily. It has rarely appeared in print, but it merits being more widely known as it is a useful knot to have at one's fingertips when faced with tying slippery, synthetic lines.

1 Make a bight in one of the two lines to be joined and bring the working end of the other line over it.

2 Tuck the working end down through the bight and bring it out to the left (in this instance), then take it over both bight legs and, in a snaking "Z" track, back again beneath them.

3 Lay the end back over its preceding part (the "over" of the knot name).

4 From the outside of the bight, tuck the working end up and through and finally lay it alongside its own standing part. Tighten gradually, working the slack out of the completed knot.

Simple Simon Under

This is a variation of the simple Simon over knot by Harry Asher. Although on first appearance, it does not look unlike the simple Simon over, it is more secure and can cope with dissimilar cord sizes and textures. This is an extremely useful knot that deserves more recognition as it is useful for slippery synthetic cord and should be used on a wider scale than it is at present.

1 Make a bight in one of the two lines to be joined and bring the working end of the other line over it.

2 Tuck the working end down through the bight and divert it to the left (in this instance) prior to going back over both bight legs.

3 Bring the working end back beneath both bight legs and then tuck it beneath its preceding part (the "under" of the knot name).

4 From the outside of the bight, tuck the working end up through and finally lay it alongside its own standing part. Tighten gradually, working the slack out of the completed knot.

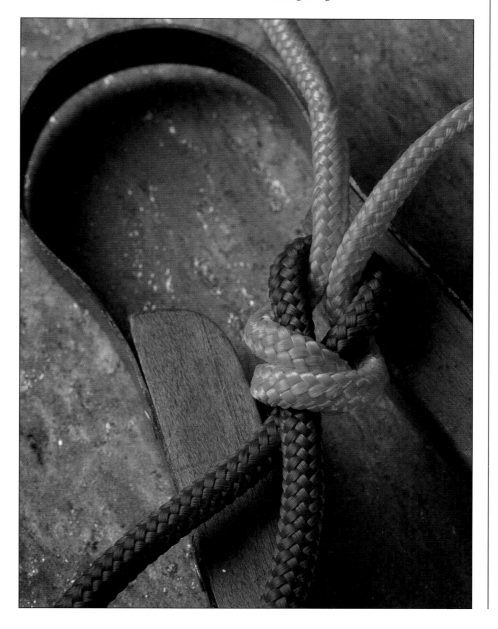

Simple Simon Double

This is a variation of the simple Simon knots of Harry Asher; it is even more secure and has the advantage that it can cope with a greater dissimilarity of cord sizes and textures.

1 Make a bight in the larger of the two lines to be joined and bring the working end of the other line over it.

2 Divert the working end (in this instance taking it to the left) beneath the bight.

3 Wrap the end over and then beneath both bight legs.

4 Take the working end back again so that it lies over both legs of the bight.

5 Pass the working end down beneath the bight over its own preceding standing part.

6 Carry the end across the front of the bight over its own standing part.

7 From the outside of the bight, finally tuck the working end through alongside its own standing part. Pull the knot snug and tight, taking care not to distort it in the process.

Shake Hands

This excellent knot is almost unknown, yet it is one of the best bends, being not only secure but also easily loosened and untied, and neat in appearance with the ends alongside the standing parts. Harry Asher devised it, influenced – admittedly – by Clifford Ashley's 1944 description of a similar layout as a loop knot.

1 Make a loop with one working end going over its own standing part.

2 Pass the other working end up through the initial loop and make a second loop (the end going under the standing part).

3 Take the first working end back down behind both of the loops in the developing knot.

4 Bring the first working end up through the common central space between both loops.

5 Now bring the first working end down in front of both loops.

6 Then tuck the second working end down through the common central space between both of the loops.

7 Pull on both working ends and standing parts in turn to tighten the knot.

Tumbling Thief Knot, Centre-tucked

This chunky knot, with both ends centrally nipped, is a good reason to learn the unreliable common thief knot described below.

1 Make a bight in one of the two lines to be joined. Bring the working end of the other line up through the bight and then divert it to the side of the bight where its short end is located.

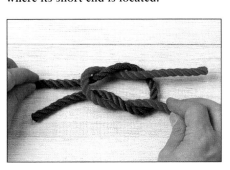

2 Bring the working end down beneath both legs of the bight, and tuck the end back through the initial bight alongside its own standing part. This is the common thief knot.

3 Now begin to pull each of the working ends across to the opposite side of the knot.

4 Uncross the working cords to momentarily assume the loosely locked layout shown.

5 Cross the two working ends over precisely as shown. This is the tumbling thief, a relatively secure form of the thief knot if drawn tight.

6 Take the upper working end and tuck it directly down through the common central space of the existing knot.

7 Take the lower working end and tuck it up through the common central space. Pull on each one of the four cords in turn to tighten this knot.

Alpine Butterfly Bend

A lot of loop knots can be converted to useful bends by cutting off the loop, and knot tyers who have spotted and reported this principle include Brion Toss, Desmond Mandeville and Harry Asher. This particular bend is derived from the Alpine butterfly knot (not described in this volume).

1 Form an underhand loop with one of the two ends to be joined.

2 Form a similar underhand loop with the other end, interlocking it with the first loop, as shown.

3 Take either one of the two working ends and tuck it down through the central space common to both loops.

4 Then tuck the other working end down beside the first end, through the almost completed knot.

5 Pull gently on both working ends, then on the standing parts, to remove slack and tighten the knot.

Vibration-proof Hitch

The American physicist Amory Bloch Lovins invented this knot over 20 years ago. It is designed for an anchorage of large diameter. Vibration of the standing part will only tighten it further due to the ratchet-like operation of the knot parts.

1 Pass the working end of the cord up, around and down the foundation from front to back, then take it diagonally up and to the right (in this instance) beneath its own standing part.

2 Take the end once more up, over and down behind the foundation.

3 Take the end across the front of the standing part then through the underlying diagonal (from left to right).

4 Go over the overlaying knot part and finally tuck the end beneath the diagonal again. Pull intermittently upon the standing part to tighten this knot.

Highwayman's Hitch

Children like to learn and show off this hitch, because of the way its apparent complexity melts to nothing with one tug on the short end. Use it as a third hand for handiwork, as well as to moor or tether a boat or horse. There is no reason to believe that highway-men ever actually used this knot.

1 Make a bight in one end of a rope, cord or other line and pass it up behind the hitching rail.

2 Pick up the standing part of the line and make a similar second bight at the front of the rail.

3 Tuck the second bight from front to back through the first one, then pull down on the working end to secure it.

4 Make a second bight in the working end (this is the third bight in total).

5 Tuck this third bight from front to back through the second one and finally pull down on the standing part to secure it. The final bight may be loaded; and the working end tugged for quick release.

Clinging Clara

When the need arises to attach a thin line to a thicker rope for a lengthwise pull, this hitch really grips and holds. It is another creation by Harry Asher, dating from about 1989. The load must be applied to the standing part, which is on the right in the step pictures (taken upwards in the finished shot). Be prudent. Leave a longer working end than the one illustrated in the step-by-step tying shots.

1 Take a turn with the working end of the smaller line around the larger rope, in the direction of the strands if it is hawser-laid.

2 Bring the working end back towards the standing part of the thinner line.

3 Lead the working end across in front of the standing part, then around behind it, to return and pass over its own previous part.

4 Take the working end (in this instance, from right to left) over one knot part, finally tucking it beneath the initial turn.

Ossel Hitch

"Ossel" is a Scottish sea fisherman's word (Cornish: "orsel") for a gill net. These knots secured the submerged lower ends of ossel lines that supported the nets as they were towed through choppy seas behind the fishing vessels known as drifters. Subjected to continual underwater movement, this seemingly simple knot coped with it all. It is a super little hitch.

1 Bring the working end down behind the foundation rope and around to the front.

2 Pass the end up and around the back of the standing part (in this instance, from left to right).

3 Take the working end down the front of the foundation rope and then bring it back up behind the work.

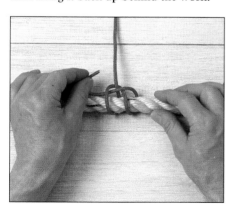

4 Finally, tuck the end over the first knot part and then beneath the second (as shown).

Boom Hitch

This attractive and robust hitch, described by Clifford Ashley in 1944, is quickly and easily tied with consecutive wrapping turns, and just a final single tuck to secure it. It really would, as the name suggests, cope with the variable direction and strength of pull involved as an improvised main sheet on a sailing dinghy, and it works equally well whether wet or dry.

1 Lay the working end diagonally up and across (in this instance, from left to right) the anchorage point.

2 Take the end down behind the anchorage and bring it under and forward again.

3 Lead the working end diagonally up and across its own standing part from right to left.

4 Take the end down again behind the anchorage and bring it forward.

5 Make a diagonal pass with the working end up and across from left to right over the intervening knot part.

6 Pass the end down behind the work between the two existing knot parts, to emerge at the front.

7 Take the end diagonally up from right to left over the standing end and one knot part.

8 Pass the working end down behind the anchorage to emerge at the front once again.

9 Make a final diagonal pass with the working end up from left to right, going over one knot part and tucking beneath the next. Make snug and tight.

Icicle Hitch

John Smith first demonstrated this astonishng contrivance to great applause in May 1990 at the eighth Annual General Meeting of the International Guild of Knot Tyers, when he hung suspended by his invention from a splicing fid (tapered point down). As this demonstration proved, with careful arrangement this remarkable hitch will hold a considerable load on the smoothest of foundations – even a fireman's brass pole would be suitable. It has more recently received fulsome praise from a civil engineer, who used it to lever a young tree out of the ground, after countless previous efforts by other means had failed and left the tree stripped of its bark and consequently slippery and smooth.

1 Lead the working end of the line over and around the foundation from front to back.

2 Take a round turn with the working end, working away from the direction of intended pull.

3 Create at least four turns, or more if an exceptionally secure hitch is required.

4 Drape the working end over the end of the foundation, as shown, with a bight hanging down at the back.

5 Bring the bight up in front of all the wrapping turns and both ends of the line, then pass it over the end of the foundation. Tighten everything by pulling each end in turn at right angles to the spar. Then tighten it again. Carefully apply the load, so that the knot stretches out (as illustrated). The final two turns – on the thicker part, if there is a taper – must not separate; if they do, add extra turns; once they remain together, the hitch should hold.

Lighterman's Hitch

River Thames tugmen tow the Port of London's heavy dumb barges (lighters) with this strong, yet versatile hitch. It has also proved its worth with riggers in circus and theatre, as well as stevedores (longshoremen), being a heavy-duty professional holdfast that would support the weight of a massive marquee or berth an ocean liner. Yet, because this hitch never completely tightens, it is remarkably adaptable as it can be cast off effortlessly in seconds.

1 Pass the working end of the tow line or guy line around the post or peg.

2 Complete a round turn, using the friction gained to check or snub the load, and adjust the rope or other line to the required length.

3 Take hold of the working end (which must be fairly long) and pull out a bight from it.

4 Bring the bight beneath the taut standing part of the line and place it over the towing post, tent peg or other anchorage point.

5 Bring the working end over the top of the standing part, creating a small loop around it.

6 Take a turn around the post or peg with the working end.

Palomar Knot

This is a strong knot, claimed by some to be 95 to 100 per cent efficient. It can be used to attach a bight securely to an angler's arbor, or to a hook, lure, swivel or sinker.

1 Pass the end of a loop (or a bight of line) through the ring.

2 Bring the bight back across itself to form a doubled loop.

3 Then tuck the bight through the loop to tie an overhand knot around the ring.

4 Push the ring itself down through the bight in the line.

5 Then carry the bight back clear over the knot parts.

Jansik Special

This is another very strong attachment (some anglers claim that it is 95 to 100 per cent) for hook, line or swivel. The double turn through the ring gives additional strength, while the triple tuck with the tag end lends security to this compact knot. It is worth perfecting this knot on thicker cord before trying to tie it in nylon monofilament.

1 Pass the working end through the ring and under the standing part.

2 Lead the end through the ring a second time to create a round turn.

3 Take the working end beneath the standing part of the line.

4 Take a wrapping turn with the working end to enclose the two earlier turns that include the standing part.

5 Tuck the working end through the loop a second time, taking care to wrap away from the ring.

6 Complete three or four turns before carefully removing all of the slack to tighten the knot.

KNOTS

"He would lie in bed all morning . . .
practising knots with the cord he kept
by his bedside."
(Mervyn Peake – Gormenghast, 1950)

The word "knot" has a specific meaning,
apart from its general use for any cordage
entanglement. Strictly speaking, it refers
only to those that are not bends or hitches,
namely stopper knots, shortenings, loops and
bindings, as well as anything tied in string
or other small stuff, such as cotton or thread.
Stopper cordage knots may be used to prevent
fraying (when a whipping cannot be applied
immediately) but their function is primarily
to prevent the cord pulling out of a pulley-
block, fairlead or other opening. Shortenings
are temporary devices, intended
to avoid cutting rope that must later be reused.
Loops may be single or multiple, fixed or
sliding. Bindings can be makeshift quick
seizings or semi-permanent lashings,
while slide-and-grip knots are remarkable
shock-absorbing contrivances.

Prusik Knot

Dr Karl Prusik, an Austrian professor of music, originally devised this knot during the First World War to mend the broken strings of musical instruments. Then, in 1931, he published instructions for mountaineers as to how it might be used for self-rescue. With downward pressure, the knot jams, but when the weight is removed, it frees itself and can be pushed up the rope. The original knot has been largely superseded by many other slide-and-grip knots, all now referred to as prusiking knots.

1 Make a bight with part of an endless sling. Lay this over a climbing rope.

2 Bend the bight over and down behind the climbing rope.

3 Pass the standing part of the sling through the working bight.

4 Pull some slack out of the initial bight and take it up and over the rope once more.

5 Take the working bight back down behind the climbing rope again.

6 Tuck the remainder of the standing part through the wrapped bight and tighten the knot.

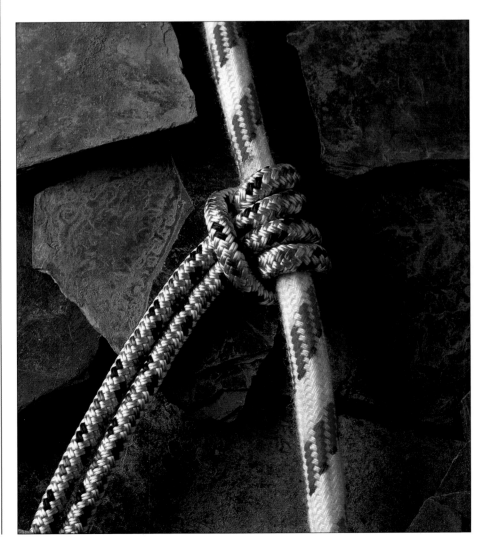

Double Prusik Knot

In icy or muddy conditions, you need to insure against slippage and modify the basic prusik knot with another wrap or two. As with the prusik knot, this can be used in pairs on one piece of rope so that it is possible to work your way up a line by alternating the weight between the two knots. Always tie the knot with cord that is smaller than the main rope it is being tied around. The double prusik knot can be adapted into an eight-wrap (triple prusik) knot – simply repeat steps 1–3.

1 Tie a basic prusik knot and pull some slack from the working bight.

2 Wrap the slack from the bight up and over the climbing rope.

3 Tuck the working bight down behind the rope to add an extra pair of wrapping turns. Tuck the working loop down through to complete the knot.

4 Tighten the result into a six-wrap version of the basic four-wrap knot. Repeat steps 1 – 3 to produce an eight-wrap (triple prusik) knot.

Bachmann Knot

Used with a karabiner, this knot can be moved more easily than the original prusik knot. It is the oldest of the so-called semi-mechanical knots that rely for their function upon the incorporation of climbing hardware.

1 Make a bight in part of an endless sling or strop.

2 Clip a karabiner into the bight, and then pass the sling behind the climbing rope.

3 Start to seize the karabiner to the rope with a wrapping turn made in the sling.

4 Add further wrapping turns, keeping them neatly alongside one another.

5 Continue to wrap until the karabiner is full (but not overfull).

Klemheist Knot

This knot may also be formed around a karabiner (not illustrated), which makes it easier to shift when prusiking.

1 Make a bight in part of an endless strop or sling.

2 Begin to wrap the sling upwards around the climbing rope.

3 Continue to create wrapping turns with the sling around the rope.

4 Ensure that both legs of the sling remain flat and parallel, with no crossovers, as the wrapping proceeds.

5 Complete four or five turns with the sling around the rope.

6 Tighten and neaten the wrapping turns (not perfectly illustrated) and bring the working bight down to the standing part of the sling.

7 Tuck the remainder of the sling through the working bight to complete this friction hitch.

Mariner's Knot

To take the weight of a fallen climber off the belay device, a sling with a mariner's knot is attached to the anchors (and a klemheist to the climbing rope). The knot can be released under load, and works best with 1.4 cm/ $^7/_{12}$ in to 1.7 cm/$^7/_{10}$ in webbing. It is, presumably, named after its originator and has no nautical use.

1 Make a flattened bight in a webbing sling of appropriate width for the size of karabiner.

2 Pass the webbing bight over and through the appropriate karabiner.

3 Tuck the sling through the karabiner a second time to create a round turn.

4 Bring the working end of the sling around the front of the standing part.

5 Wrap it around the back of the standing part of the sling.

6 Wrap a second, third and fourth turn around the standing part.

7 Finally, tuck the working end of the sling between the two flat legs of the standing part. Friction and tension alone secure this hitch.

Penberthy Knot

Devised by Larry Penberthy and Dick Mitchell in about 1969, this prusiking knot is also known as the caver's helical knot. As it can be fiddly to tie, climbing writer Bill March suggests a sling weighted with a karabiner twirled around the rope, and the sling then threaded through it, makes tying much easier. Always adjust the number of turns and the amount of slack to the user's weight; too much slack and it slips, too little and it becomes difficult to shift.

1 Use a suitable size of accessory cord for the climbing rope.

2 Begin to wrap turns around the rope; it may not matter whether the turns go up (as illustrated) or down.

3 Wrap the accessory cord a second time around the climbing rope.

4 Continue until five or six wrapping turns have been completed.

5 Make an overhand loop in the upper one of the two cords.

6 Then take the lower cord and tuck it through this loop.

7 Take the working end (lower end of the cord) around the upper cord of the half-completed knot.

8 Tuck the end down through the loop to secure the arrangement with a sheet bend.

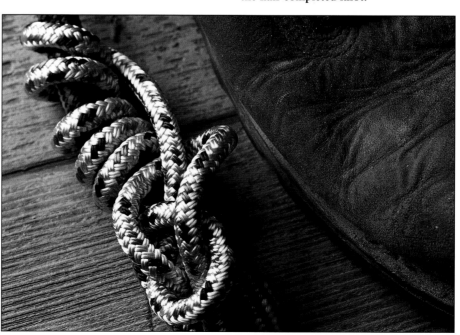

Heddon Knot

This knot, which was invented by Chet Heddon in 1959, is also referred to as a cross-prusik knot and as a kreuzklem. It is rated about as effective as the original prusik knot, is harder to loosen and may be tied in either accessory cord or webbing. Avoid tying it upside down or it will slip and not hold. This knot seems to be used only by climbers, but there is no reason why it should not be adopted for mundane use on level ground.

1 Make a bight in a cord or webbing sling and use single or doubled climbing rope.

2 Pass the sling bight behind the climbing rope, then bring it back in front of it.

3 Wrap the other end of the sling across the front of its own bight and around the back of the rope.

4 Finally, tuck the longer sling bight down through the initial bight.

Double Heddon Knot

This elaboration of the basic Heddon, cross-prusik or kreuzklem knot generates greater friction and so may be expected to cope with a greater load. The extra wrap of this beefed-up version of the heddon gives it a slightly different appearance, and this makes it somewhat harder to loosen before it can fulfil its slide-and-grip role, but it is nevertheless a useful variation.

1 Make a bight in a cord or webbing sling and use single or doubled climbing rope.

2 Pass the bight behind the rope, then wrap the remainder of the sling around the rope to trap the bight. Take the sling round to the back of the rope.

3 Wrap the long end of the sling across the front of its own bight a second time and take it once more around the back of the rope.

4 Finally, tuck the longer sling bight down through the initial bight.

Release Hitch, Top Loaded

To overcome the shortcomings of other prusiking knots, Robert Chisnall came up with this innovation around 1980. A weight on the load end causes the turns around the abseil (rappel) line to tighten and the knot to grip. A sharp tug on the release end causes first the top and then the other wrapping turns to slide. Care must be taken in tying this knot as, if it is at all sloppy or loose, it will slip before jamming and may fail.

1 Tie figure-of-eight loops in both ends of a length of cord. Arrange one end, knot down, alongside the climbing rope; then make an overhand loop with the other end.

2 Take the working end around the back of the rope and bring it up through its own loop.

3 Make another wrapping turn with the working end around the rope and up through the loop.

4 Complete as many wrapping turns as may be necessary for the required friction, then pull on the lower end to tighten the knot.

Release Hitch, Bottom Loaded

The bottom loaded version of this hitch, by contrast, is more secure than the prusik knot. It will grip even when sloppily tied, although it tends to drift apart when loaded if there is any slack. The trade-off is that the release end then has to be pulled very hard to make it slip. When tied neatly, the bottom loaded release hitch can be freed more easily.

1 Tie figure-of-eight loops in both ends of a length of accessory cord.

2 Arrange one end of the cord, knot down, alongside the climbing rope; then make an overhand loop as shown with the other end.

3 Lead the working end of the accessory cord around the back of the climbing rope.

4 Tuck the working end up through its earlier loop from front to back, and lead it around behind the rope.

5 Make the first of several wrapping turns to enclose both the cord and rope together.

6 Complete as many wrapping turns as necessary for the required friction.

7 Bring the working end out through the knot as shown and pull upon the unused end to tighten it.

Extended French Prusik Knot

This is another Robert Chisnall innovation from around 1981. It is a sort of Chinese finger trap, in which the extension brought about by a load reduces its diameter, so that it clings to the rope around which it is wrapped. To shift it by hand, grasp the upper end and pull down, thus shortening it and increasing its diameter, so that it releases its grip and slides. In fact, it is intentional that this knot slides under a shock loading as it absorbs energy until the falling load is low enough for the sling and rope to withstand, when it will grip and hold, thus making it ideal for climbers. This tape knot works equally well on a single or doubled climbing rope.

1 Middle a length of 25 mm/1 in tubular tape and arrange it with the bight around the climbing rope.

2 Lead both ends in opposite spirals around the rope, crossing one over the other when they meet.

3 Take both working lengths around to the back of the rope, where the one that went over at the previous crossing point now goes under.

4 Bring the tapes around to the front again, alternating the crossover once more.

5 Continue with this over-under-over wrapping of the tape around the rope.

6 Keep the diamond spaces between the tapes as small as possible.

7 Eight or ten wrapping turns are sufficient for this innovative knot.

8 Tie a pair of figure-of-eight loops as close to the rope as possible to be held by a karabiner.

Chi-Fi Knot

This variation of the extended French prusik knot, named after Canadian climbers Robert Chisnall and Jean-Marc Filion, is tied in an endless sling. It frees the user's hands for abseil (rappel) and rescue work. It is a close relation of the extended French prusik knot, also devised by Robert Chisnall. This clever slide-and-grip knot appeared first in the 1989 *Safety Manual* of the Ontario Rock Climbing Association, and may be unknown outside its membership. It is nevertheless a remarkable friction device that could prove useful in all kinds of situations. Aboard boats, the karabiner could be replaced by a shackle and pin. NOTE – This knot glazes slings, losing friction. Retire if glazing is apparent, and in any case after 10 to 12 uses in this way.

1 Place a tape sling around the climbing rope (which may be single or doubled), crossing one length of rope over the other.

2 Take both sections of tape around to the back of the rope, alternating the crossover.

3 Continue to wrap the tapes, with alternating crossovers, ensuring that the diamond spaces between the tapes are kept as small as possible.

4 Wrap the tapes until all of the slack in the sling is used up.

5 Neaten the lower half of the knot, until it matches the top half, and clip a karabiner through the two remaining bights.

Chinese Lanyard Knot

Less difficult to tie than it appears at first glance, the unusual square shape and texture of this knot make the result worth the effort. It can be used as a decorative means of holding two pieces of cord together – ideal for a necklace. Chinese knotting writer Lydia Chen calls this the plafond knot (*plafond* meaning decorated ceiling) because it resembles the motifs seen in Chinese temples and palaces.

1 Middle a length of cord and make a narrow bight in it.

2 Tie a half-knot with both ends of the cord length.

3 Tie an identical second half-knot to complete a loose granny knot.

4 Leave a gap of 7–8 cm/about 3 in and tie a second identical granny knot.

5 Invert the lower granny knot, turning it bottom-for-top.

6 Similarly invert the top granny knot, turning it top-for-bottom.

7 Tuck the original bight down through the centre of the lower granny knot.

8 Tuck the lefthand one of the two working ends up through the centre of the upper granny knot.

9 Turn the almost completed knot face down and bring the new lefthand working end out to the front.

10 Finally, tuck the lefthand working end up through the upper granny knot. Ensure that the loop is long enough to go over the object it will hold, then patiently remove the slack from this knot (slowly does it), working towards both working ends.

Chinese Button Knot

This is a classic button knot that can be stitched to a bag or purse and serves either as an attractive fastening or a decorative accessory. Knotted buttons tend to be too large for buttonholes, so fasten them with cord loops or frogs. Tied with craft and patience in very small fine material, button knots make unusual earrings. In some stiff materials, this knot can be made to stay flat, for ornamentation rather than practicality.

1 Middle – more or less – a short length of decorative cord.

3 Then pass the working end down behind the loop just formed.

2 With one end of the cord make an overhand loop.

4 Pick up the other end and tuck it (in this instance, from left to right) under-over-under-over; keep hold of the partially formed knot, as this is not a locking tuck.

5 Finally lead the later working end up and down through the knot as shown.

Prise up as knot tightens

6 Arrange the four-lobed symmetrical knot with the two standing cord parts as a stem, then gradually remove the slack until the knot becomes convex like a mushroom. As it tightens, the central knot part (indicated in the illustration) will tend to recede from sight and must be prised up to the surface of the knot where it will then remain.

Chinese Button Knot (Doubled)

The Chinese button knot is often doubled to produce a bulkier and therefore showier knot. When making this version, it is not necessary to prise up the top central part, which is supported by underlying strands.

1 Continue from step 6 of the Chinese button knot and bring the two working ends alongside one another.

2 Begin to follow the original lead with one of them.

3 Using the other end, start to follow the original lead around in the opposite direction.

4 Continue with both ends until the single-ply knot is entirely doubled.

5 Tuck the ends down through the centre of the knot and carefully tighten it.

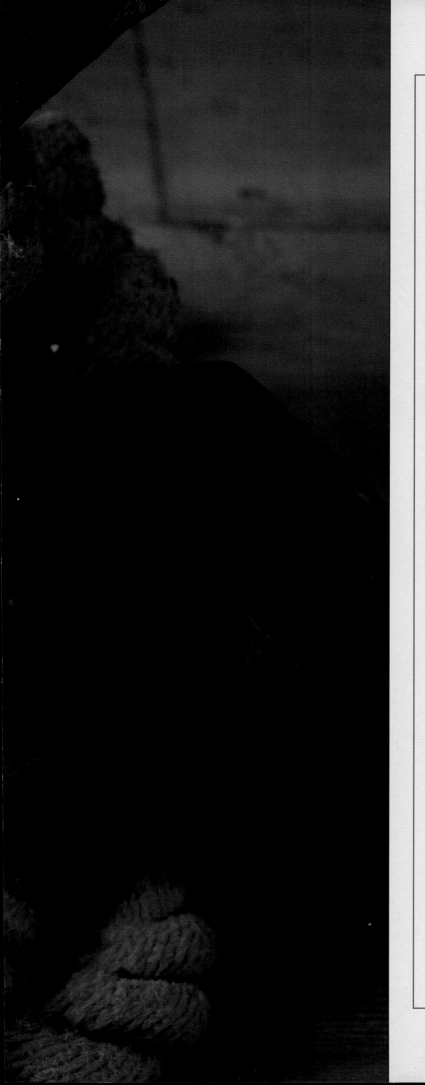

BINDINGS & LOOPS

"I might give up my life for my friend, but he had better not ask me to do up a parcel."
(LOGAN PEARSALL SMITH, 1865-1946)

There are two kinds of binding knot. The first is around an object with a wide diameter, where a cord, strap or fabric is wound one or more times and the two ends are then securely tied together (for example, packing parcels, securing a cloth covering to a homemade jar of preserves or applying a first aid tourniquet). The second is for narrow diameters, when a special constricting knot is applied to grip and hold with its own internal friction (for example, to prevent the cut end of a rope from fraying or to attach a hose to a tap). A loop knot may be used like a hitch, but placed over a post or rail (rather than tied around it), the advantage being that it is easily removed again for re-use. Double and multiple loops are for improvised working hoists and rescue slings (in the absence of better alternatives). Running knots or nooses, useful for parcels, may have originated as snares to catch animals and birds for food. Some loops are tied in the bight, others in the end of the cordage that is being used.

Boa Knot

This robust binding was devised and announced in 1996 by the accomplished weaver Peter Collingwood, who wanted a knot that would remain securely in place when the foundation around which it was tied was cut close alongside the knot. It is similar to the strangle knot in structure and qualities but is an even more secure arrangement. It is also quick and easy to tie, and these two factors have ensured its prompt adoption by many discerning knot tyers.

1 Make an overhand loop with a short length of the chosen material.

2 Add a similar second turn on top of the first one.

3 Arrange these turns in the form of a coil with both ends lying in the same direction; there should be three cord parts under each thumb.

4 Rotate the righthand side of this coil through 180°, as shown (that is, to put the bottom where the top had been).

5 Check that the resulting figure-of-eight has three knot parts around each loop and in the overlaying diagonal, with just two parts underneath.

6 Begin to insert the rope, rod or whatever is to be seized, beneath one or other of the end loops.

7 Continue by sliding the foundation over the centre crossing, which totals five knot parts.

8 Push it carefully through the far loop, when the knot will be completely held upon it.

9 Finally, work this knot snugly into shape, with three twined knot parts overlaid by a pair of diagonals. The ends may be cut much shorter than shown.

Asher's Equalizer

This cunning knot, added to a jug (pitcher), jar or bottle sling (p. 86), adjusts loop lengths automatically to give two handles the same size, and makes the object much easier to carry. It was devised by Harry Asher.

1 Ensure the completed jug (pitcher), jar or bottle sling has two long ends and a shorter loop.

2 Start to pull the two long ends a short way through the loop until they create twin bights.

3 Bring the single large loop formed by the knotted ends over the twin bights just formed.

4 Pull the twin bights completely through the single large loop.

5 Tighten the resulting knot to create a pair of matching handles.

Double Figure-of-Eight Hitch

Owen K. Nuttall of West Yorkshire, England came across this binding knot in the 1980s. It is arguably one of the best binding knots for security. The attraction of this particular form is the easily acquired and memorized double figure-of-eight layout. Try it as an alternative to the boa and strangle knots.

1 First make a clockwise overhand loop with one end of a length of cord or twine.

2 Add an anticlockwise (counterclockwise) overhand loop to form a figure-of-eight.

3 Lay a second clockwise overhand loop on top of the first one.

4 Pick up the other end and place another clockwise overhand loop atop the remaining single loop.

5 Begin to slide the knot over its intended core, or insert the core through the knot, as shown.

6 Locate the knot where required on and around the object to be seized.

7 Pull on both ends as hard as possible to tighten this binding knot.

Jug, Jar or Bottle Sling

The interwoven knot parts of this clever contrivance will cling unyieldingly to the narrow neck of a bottle, providing it has a very slight, narrow lip, or provide substantial carrying handles for a larger jug or jar (pitcher) – even an ancient Greek amphora. Use it to cool picnic wine in a mountain stream, to lug a churn of milk across the farmyard or to suspend a hanging basket of flowers from a kitchen beam.

1 Roughly middle an appropriate length of strong cord and make a long bight.

2 Bend the bight down to create two matching long loops.

3 Overlap the two loops of cord by laying the righthand one upon the lefthand one.

4 Locate the section of cord that overlays both legs of the original bight and begin to pull it up beneath the existing layout.

5 Pull out a bight and make a locking tuck with it over-and-under through the overlapped loops.

6 Extend the working bight about 7 cm/2¾ in beyond the half-completed knot.

7 Take hold of the large curving loop at the back of the knot.

8 Then pull it down to touch the two standing parts of the cord.

9 Take hold of the similar large curving loop at the front of the knot.

10 Pull this loop down too until it touches the two standing parts of the cord.

11 Tug gently and experimentally on both bight and cord legs until the tension is evenly distributed throughout the resulting braided bracelet of a knot.

12 Place the knot around the neck of the chosen jug (pitcher), jar or bottle and pull the outer loops as tight as possible.

13 Insert one of the long ends through the shorter loop, then tie the two ends together with a fisherman's knot or other secure bend, to create two self-adjusting handles that will always be the same length when held.

Square Turk's Head (4 Lead x 5 Bight)

This Turk's head knot has four interwoven strands (or leads) with five scallop-shaped rim parts (bights). These dimensions give it a shorthand label: it is known as a 4-lead x 5-bight Turk's head (abbreviated further when written to 4L x 5B TH). All Turk's heads that have just one lead more or less than the number of bights are also referred to as "square" Turk's heads. This tying method was developed by Charlie Smith.

1 Middle a length of cord and lead the working end around the base of the thumb, over the standing part, to go (from front to back) between the first and second fingers.

2 Take the end around the forefinger, then up through (under-and-over) the thumb loop, and beneath the standing part.

3 Now lead the working end between the second and third fingers, and around the second finger, to tuck under one/over two/under one (as illustrated).

4 Pass the end over the standing part and between the third and little fingers, returning between the second and third fingers and tucking up through the second finger loop.

5 Lead the working end, in a final satisfactory locking tuck, over/under/over/under/over, and then tuck the end up alongside the standing part, as shown.

6 The completed knot may remain flattened, or be turned into a bracelet, and (in form) doubled or tripled by following the original lead around with the surplus cord of the unused standing end. The main picture shows a tripled bracelet.

Square Turk's Head (5 Lead x 4 Bight)

Use this single-strand Turk's head instead of perfected whipping to seize the cut ends of ropes. A square Turk's head like this makes a pretty but practical sliding sleeve for the drawcord on a duffel bag. Then again, it can embellish anything it will fit, from bellropes and handrails to key fobs or the gear shift of a classic sports car.

1 Middle a length of cord and pass the working end over and down behind the core, to reappear on the right of the standing part. Go diagonally up (from right to left) over the previous lead.

2 Take the end over, around and down behind the core, emerging to the immediate right of the standing part, tucking over one/under one/ over one, from right to left.

3 Lead the working end down behind the core, to reappear again just to the right of the standing part, and tuck (left to right) under one/over one.

4 Rotate the work, bringing the rear side into view, and tuck the end (right to left) over/under/over.

5 Turn the work back to its original position and tuck the working end to the right of the standing part (and left to right) over/under/over.

6 Rotate the work, to show the rear side. Lead the end (right to left) in a final locking tuck under/over/under/over.

7 Place the working end alongside the standing part to complete the knot, which may then be doubled and tripled by following around the original lead with the surplus cord.

Twined Turk's Head (2 Lead x 3 Bight)

This primitive version of a Turk's head is unusual. It is rarely seen, although it has been used to bind the ends of hunting crops.

1 Tie an overhand knot around the chosen core with the working end of a length of cord.

2 Lead the end over, around and down behind the core, to reappear to the right of the standing part.

3 Tuck the working end alongside the standing part and parallel to it.

4 Follow the original lead with the working end, tucking under and staying parallel to it (on the same side).

5 Continue to reproduce the original lead, doubling the knot with the working end.

6 Tuck the working end under the next loop, following the standing part as before.

7 Tuck the working end in to complete. Make a 2L x 3B TH this way. With an initial double overhand knot, produce a 2L x 5B TH. A treble overhand knot results in a 2L x 7B TH. A quadruple overhand knot creates a 2L x 9B TH, and so on.

Spade End Knot

Anglers attach monofilament to spade-ended (eyeless) hooks, or short leader lengths to thicker lines, with this knot. It is akin to perfected whipping.

1 Make a loop in the thinner stuff and arrange it so that the short end is alongside the thicker line.

2 Leaving the short end in position, begin to wrap the body of the loop, enclosing and holding both parts of itself as well as the thicker line.

3 Continue to bind tightly, with each succeeding turn snugly up against the preceding one.

4 Complete about 2 cm/⅝ in of wrapping, then pass the shrunken loop over the end of the thicker line.

5 Remove any remaining slack from the bight, then pull in opposite directions on both ends to tighten.

Angler's Loop

This is an old angling knot, from the 17th-century days of Sir Izaak Walton and lines made of gut, which has resurfaced as a secure loop knot for the latest manmade ropes. It will even stay tied in bungee (elasticated) shock cord. This knot too can be tied in the bight, but the method illustrated is easier to learn and remember.

1 Immobilize the end of the line and make an overhand loop with the standing part.

2 Bring the end over and lay it across the initial loop.

3 Pull a bight through to create what is, at this stage, an overhand knot with a drawloop.

4 Lead the working end around behind the standing part of the line.

5 Tuck the end through the centre of the knot, trapping it neatly beneath the two legs of the loop.

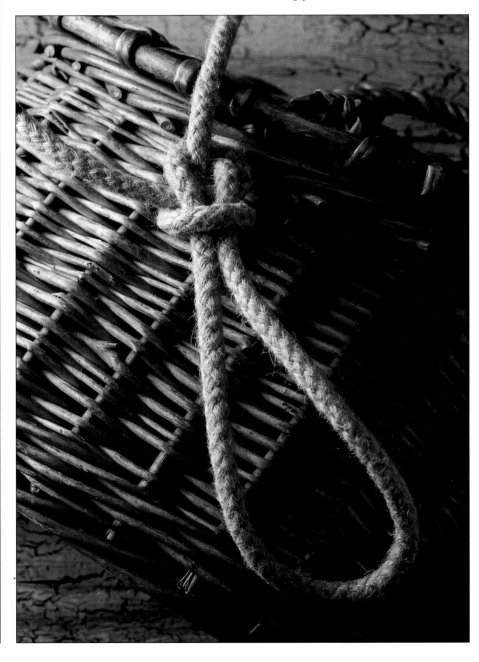

Frost Knot

The Frost knot is just a simple overhand loop that is tied in webbing. This is used in the improvised short lengths of climbing ladders called étriers (French: stirrups). It was devised by Tom Frost some time in the 1960s. This has essentially been created for use as a tape knot, and is not, therefore, generally tied in cordage.

1 Make a short bight in one end of a length of webbing or tape and insert the other end between the two flat sections of the bight.

2 Form an anticlockwise (counter-clockwise) overhand loop with all three parts of the webbing or tape.

3 Take the bight and its extra end around behind the loop and pull them through to tie what is in effect a compound overhand knot.

4 Tighten the completed knot, taking care to keep all three sections flat and together.

Double Frost Knot

In combination with the basic Frost knot, this variation of its simple relative improvises the foot loops in étriers (short webbing ladders).

1 Make matching bights in two suitable lengths of climbing webbing.

2 Form one of the two bights into an overhand loop.

3 Then complete the tying of a simple overhand knot with the bight.

4 Insert the other bight through the knot to lie on top of the first bight.

5 Follow the lead of the knotted first bight with the second one.

6 Ensure, as the knot is progressively doubled, that all of the webbing parts lie flat together.

7 Tighten the completed knot, leaving twin loops of the required size.

Double Figure-of-Eight

This double looped knot, popular with climbers, was described in 1944 by Clifford Ashley. It is tied in the bight. A useful characteristic of this knot is the absence of any ends that might work loose, which helps to make it relatively secure. The twin loops generally tend to emerge the same size. If each one must be a different length for it to be used in particular circumstances, arrange this by patiently feeding slack line as required through the completed knot.

1 Middle the rope as required, form a bight, and with it create a clockwise underhand loop.

2 Bring the end of the bight around (from right to left) in front of the twin standing parts of the rope.

3 Take the bight down behind the loop, and then begin to pull it partially through.

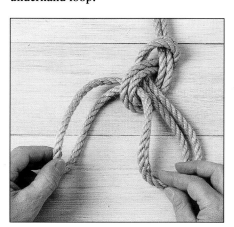

4 Adjust the emerging couple of loops to the required size.

5 Place the end of the bight over the newly formed loops.

6 Then pass the bight over the entire knot to secure the paired loops.

Blood Loop Dropper Knot

Tied in angling lines, this knot makes a strong starting loop for a paternoster tackle system, although some anglers argue that it should be limited to fly-fishing. In the much thicker cord illustrated here, it forms a useful loop in the middle of a line for all kinds of attachments.

1 Form a loop as the starting point for a triple overhand knot.

2 Tie a simple overhand knot, keeping the loop looser than illustrated.

3 Take a second tuck with one or other of the working ends.

4 Now take a third tuck to arrive at a triple overhand knot.

5 Locate the centre of the two twined knot parts and then pull the original single loop down between the two knot parts into a small bight.

6 Carefully shape and work the knot snug and tight, with the loop at the required size.

Brummycham Bowline

Neatest with just two loops, this knot may be tied with many more loops by treating it like a coil of rope. Its name is no doubt derived from the local nickname for the city of Birmingham, "Brum", where the knot's British innovator, Harry Asher, resided.

1 Double one end of a rope to create a bight no longer than the length of the intended loops.

2 Make a loop of the required size with the long end of the rope.

3 Make a second loop of the required size with the long end of the rope (add three or more loops if necessary).

4 Form an underhand loop with the long end of the rope.

5 Pass the loop over the top of the two (or more) bights.

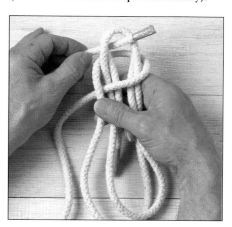

6 Pass the working end through all of the upper bights from back to front to complete this knot.

Hangman's Noose

The grisly name of this knot should not be allowed to detract from its general usefulness. It is – with the exception of the bimini twist – the ultimate strong and secure loop. The snug wrapping turns of this knot are an indication of its shock-absorbing slide-and-grip characteristics. Ensure that when applying the turns you keep them close alongside one another.

1 Form a flattened "S" or "Z" shape in the end of a length of rope or cord.

2 Begin to wrap the twin legs of the loop with the working end.

3 Take care to trap the third cordage part in the groove between the other two parts.

4 Continue to wrap the working end around the three enclosed knot parts, ensuring that all three nest close together in a triangular cross-section.

5 Ensure that each turn is made fairly tight by pulling steadily on the working end.

6 Continue to make wrapping turns with the working end, keeping them snug and tight.

7 Aim to do at least seven turns (sailors' knotlore says that the number seven represents the seven seas).

8 Finally, tuck the working end through the nearby small loop and trap it by pulling upon whichever one of the two legs of the large loop closes the other loop.

Triple Figure-of-Eight

This is yet another of those useful climbing contrivances created in the mid-1980s by Canadian Robert Chisnall.

1 Middle – or make a long bight in – the rope to be tied.

2 Make a clockwise underhand loop with the previously made bight.

3 Bring the bight over the twin standing parts from right to left.

4 Lay the working bight behind the original loop (from the left).

5 Then pull twin loops through, at the same time creating a doubled figure-of-eight layout.

6 Adjust the newly formed twin loops to the required length.

7 Finally, lead the bight over the twin standing parts, from left to right, and tuck it (back to front) through beside the existing two loops to form a third one.

Bimini Twist

This remarkably strong loop (95–100 per cent), recommended for big game fishing, has been in print since at least 1975. It is illustrated for clarity in much larger cordage than would in fact be used; consequently, it was not possible to show realistically how the hands – and feet – would actually cooperate in tying this knot with fine monofilament or braid. Still, the various stages are correctly shown. The numerous initial twists, simply imparted with a forefinger, are then spread apart to create the overlaying series of wrapping turns that strengthen and finish off this knot.

1 Make a bight over 50 cm/20 in long. Insert a finger in the end of the bight and begin to twist a loop around.

2 Impart some 20 twists to the bight, holding both parts of the line so that they do not unwind.

3 Spread the loop. In practice, this must be done with the feet, while both hands are free to control the two upper ends of the line. Start to enlarge the loop to unwind the initial twists.

4 An overriding layer of wrapping turns should appear where the hands are focused. Hold the standing part taut and feed the working end at right angles into these turns under steady tension, keeping them tight and close together.

5 With the working end, take a half hitch around one leg of the large loop.

6 Finally, make a half hitch with the working end around both legs of the loop.

Fireman's Chair Knot

One loop, adjusted for size, fits beneath the subject's armpits, with the other loop placed around the back of the knees. A rescuer then lowers the person by means of one long end, while a second rescuer pulls them away from the wall, cliff or other hazard with the lower rope. Caution must be exercised when dealing with makeshift loop knots; manufactured harnesses are usually the safest option.

1 Cast a clockwise overhand loop in the bight of the rescue rope.

2 Then add an anticlockwise (counterclockwise) underhand loop of similar size to the first one.

3 Partly overlap both loops, ensuring that the righthand one is in front of the left.

4 Pull the leading edge of the lefthand loop (from the back to the front) through the righthand loop; at the same time pull the leading edge of the righthand loop (from the front to the back) through the lefthand loop.

5 Pull on both loops at once to tighten the knot so far formed.

6 Take the lefthand standing part around the back of the lefthand loop and bring it over to the front.

7 Take the working end down through its own loop to tie a half hitch.

8 Take the righthand standing part over the top of the righthand loop and round the back.

9 Tuck the working end through its own loop from back to front to tie another half hitch.

MATS, PLAITS, RINGS, SLINGS & THINGS

"With a bit of string and a modicum of topological ingenuity it was possible to convert my long-sleeved sweater into an impromptu rucksack . . ."

(SIR FRED HOYLE – *OSSIAN'S RIDE*, 1959)

Knots are like tools. It is possible to muddle along with four or five, using and misusing them for every task imaginable. The best strategy, however, is to acquire a full and varied repertoire of bends, hitches and other contrivances, so that you always have precisely the correct combination for the job in hand. There are many knots, bends and hitches that may be used only infrequently; but, when they are, nothing else will do as well. What follows is a selection of these occasional knots.

Jury Mast Knot

With its three adjustable loops, this knot's day job was once to rig a makeshift (jury) mast in a boat. Each of the loops and the two ends made attachment points for the necessary shrouds and stays in order to steady and support it. Nowadays, it is reduced to celebrity appearances as a knot tyer's party piece.

1 Cast a clockwise overhand loop in the bight of the rope.

2 Add an anticlockwise (counterclockwise) underhand loop and partially overlap the two (lefthand loop over righthand).

3 Make another anticlockwise (counterclockwise) underhand loop, to the right of the existing couple, and partially overlap it below the centre loop.

4 Further overlap the lefthand and the righthand loops (the right over the left) within the middle loop.

5 Pull the leading edge of the righthand loop – under/over – to create a long lefthand loop.

6 Pull the leading edge of the lefthand loop over/under to produce a matching righthand loop.

7 Lastly, pull the upper edge of the centre loop up to create an upper third loop.

Poldo Tackle

This all-or-nothing tensioning contrivance is quickly assembled; pull one way to tighten, the other way to slacken off. Use it for a clothes line or as a quick-release lashing for an on-deck life raft.

1 Tie a strong and secure fixed loop (an angler's loop is illustrated) in one end of the line.

2 Tuck the other end of the line through the small fixed loop to produce a large running loop.

3 Bring the end around and make a sliding bight on the running leg of the large loop.

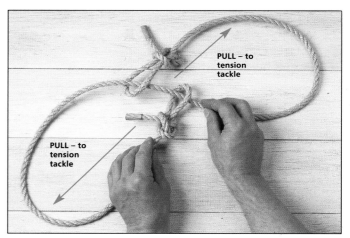

PULL – to tension tackle

PULL – to tension tackle

4 Secure the bight just made with a matching fixed loop knot. To tension the tackle, pull the two knots apart; to slacken it again, push them back together.

Monkey's Fist

Add weight where it will improve the flight and distance of a messenger or throwing line with this time-honoured knot. It needs a core to retain its shape – something heavy like a round stone, which should be inserted before completing the last three turns. Take care to throw the knotted rope's end within arm's length of the catcher (but not directly at him or her) as the core can make this knot very heavy.

1 Choose a line of appropriate weight and thickness; a line that floats is preferable for use over water.

2 Make three complete turns, working away from the short end, and hold them flat (each one beside the next).

3 Turn the line 90° and add another similar complete turn.

4 Continue to add two more complete turns. Ensure that the second set of turns lies flat and enclose the first three turns.

5 Turn the line 90° again, and tuck the end through at the top of the knot, between the two sets of turns.

6 Then tuck the end through at the bottom of the knot, between the two sets of turns.

7 Complete three final turns, at right angles to the first two sets of turns; insert a round stone, discarded squash ball or other hard filler of the right size, and painstakingly, a bit at a time, tighten all of the wrapping turns. Secure the short end to the standing part of the line with a knot or tape.

Ringbolt Hitching

With only a single cord, this hitching produces a spine running along the outer edge of the ring. This attractive finish makes it suitable for the thickest or broadest rings.

1 Take a full turn around the ring, tucking up under two cord parts at the front, before going around again and tucking up through one part.

2 Turn the working end down and tuck diagonally (from right to left) under one knot part.

3 Wrap around the front of the ring (from left to right) and pass through the ring (from right to left).

4 Describe a figure-of-eight, diagonally up (from left to right) in front of the knotwork, then directly back (from right to left) beneath two cord parts.

5 Repeat step 4, wrapping down and to the right, through the ring (from right to left), and then up and right.

6 Then tuck the end (from right to left) under two parts. Repeat this process until the entire ring is covered with the cord.

Versatackle

Devised and published in October 1985 by George Aldridge, this tackle applies tension wherever needed. It may be tied in small cord and used as an improvised clamp for newly glued picture frames, chairs or other woodwork; in rope, it will raise heavy loads, retrieve a bogged-down motor vehicle, or it can be used to tension guylines or shrouds on tents, flagpoles or radio masts. It truly is a versatile tackle – hence its name. This device can chafe loops tied in vegetable fibre ropes, but synthetic cordage will survive much longer without weakening.

1 Make a single fixed loop in the end of the cordage (an angler's loop is ideal). At a distance somewhat greater than the two fixed points to be connected, tie a second similar loop in the bight.

2 Note how the working end emerges from one side of the second loop; take this through the first loop from that same side.

3 Thread it through the second loop in the opposite direction.

4 Circling in the same direction, pass the working end through the first loop again.

5 Pass the end through the second loop, continuing the coiling pattern.

6 Take one more complete turn, so that there are three standing parts on each side of the two loops. Pull on the free end of the line to exert a powerful pull. Let go and – surprisingly – this ad hoc tackle is self-locking (but add a retaining half hitch for safety's sake). To release it, unthread the working end a tuck or two, until the entire arrangement can be loosened.

Double Ring Hitching

For rings with a thicker diameter, or those made to appear so by comparatively thin cord, this version (with a rope-like spine) may look better than the continuous ring hitching. Ring hitching may be scaled up or down and applied to many handicrafts, and it can also be applied to handles.

1 Lead the working end in a figure-of-eight around the ring, first going up and across the front of the ring (from left to right), then around the back (from right to left), down the front diagonally (from left to right), around the back again (right to left), tucking up at the front (left to right) and going under/over.

2 Pass the working end through the ring from right to left and then feed it through up to the right under two knot parts.

3 Repeat step 2, passing the end through the ring and again tucking up to the right beneath two knot parts.

4 At intervals, straighten the spine, as it tends to drift off-centre; this also tightens the knotting.

5 Continue to wrap the working end around and through the ring, always in the same direction.

6 Repeatedly tuck up and under two cord parts, until all of the foundation of the ring is covered with the cord.

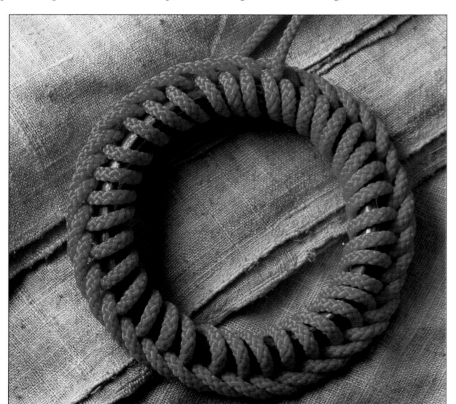

Eight-Strand Square Plait

This chunky, herringbone weave is superb for all kinds of heavier work. Inuits (Eskimos) used it to scale up fine fishing lines for catching larger sea mammals – and today it is worked in leather thongs to make sturdy leashes for large dogs. Try different coloured strands in various positions to discover the several patterns that can be made with this plait (braid).

1 Bind eight strands together and subdivide them into left and righthand groups of four; lead the outermost (and uppermost) lefthand strand – red, in this example – around and behind the work, to emerge in the middle of the four righthand strands, returning to lie inside and below the three companion strands back on its lefthand side.

2 Similarly, lead the outermost (and uppermost) righthand strand – green, in this instance – around behind the work, to emerge in the middle of the four lefthand strands, returning to lie inside and below its three partners back on its own righthand side.

3 Repeat step 1, being sure to take (as the working strand) the uppermost strand – that is, the one furthest away.

4 Repeat step 2, taking care to select (as the working strand) the one furthest away.

5 Continue with this process, always using (as the working strand) the one not used for the longest time.

6 Tighten the work as each step is completed; in particular, tension each strand as it goes around the unseen back of the work. Bind the ends together.

Diamond Hitch

Explorers, prospectors and other wilderness pioneers, dependent upon pack animals to convey all sorts of loads, once swore by this hitch, and it can still be spotted in the more authentic cowboy films. The lashing will secure irregularly shaped commodities, as they stir and strain, not only on the backs of mules and horses but also loaded on to beach buggies, snowmobiles or other motor vehicles (on or off-road). It is also ideal for human backpackers with unpackable items to carry.

1 Select a suitable length of lashing for backpack or luggage rack.

2 Secure the standing end to a centrally placed anchorage point.

3 Take the line loosely across the load, around a second anchorage opposite the first, then return.

4 Twist the two parts of the lashing together, until most of the slack is removed. Find the centre of the twist.

5 Lead the line down and around a corner lashing, then back to tuck centrally through the nearest centre side of the twisted portion of the lashing.

6 Take the line down around the next corner anchorage point.

7 Then bring it up through the central diamond that gives this hitch its distinctive name.

8 Take the line around the third anchorage point and bring it back to tuck once more through the central diamond shape.

9 Lead the line around the remaining corner anchorage, and then bring it back down to the starting point. Secure it at this point.

Simple Chain

This simple chain will shorten an over-long rope or cord by about one-third. It will also embellish a fine twine, to make an attractive cord to retain reading glasses, for example.

1 Cast an anticlockwise (counter-clockwise) overhand loop with a long working end.

2 Lay the working end beneath the loop and pull a bight (from back to front) through it; then pull the resulting knot tight.

3 Pull a second bight in the working end through the first bight and pull it tight.

4 Similarly, pull a third bight through the second bight and pull it tight.

5 Continue pulling, bight through bight, tightening each stage before going on to the next.

6 To finish the chain, simply tuck the working end through the preceding bight. This will secure the completed chain sufficiently.

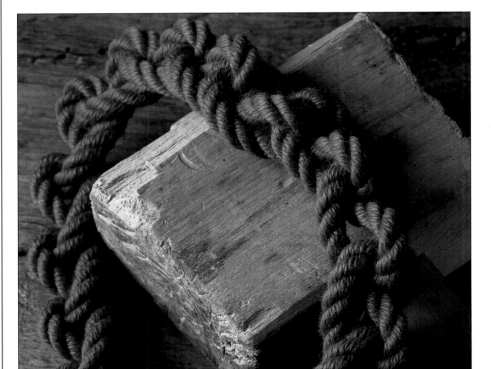

Endless Simple Chain

This is a very neat way to join the ends of a simple chain, ensuring that it keeps the same shape even on the join. It makes an original bracelet, necklace or anklet, and it may even be used to frame a picture or mirror. The steps are illustrated in two different colours but this chain is usually made with two ends of one cord.

1 Bring the beginning and end of one or two simple chains together.

2 Tuck the final end – in this instance, the lefthand one – up through the starting loop (from the back to the front), alongside the standing end.

3 Take the working end up (from the back to the front) through its own loop, beside itself.

4 Pass the end to the right, down (from front to back) through the adjacent loop made by step 3.

5 Withdraw the standing end from the first of its tucks and replace it with the working end.

Chain Stitch Lashing

This lashing uses more line than many others, but it fits nicely over lumpy and bumpy long parcels, with the dividend that it can be readily undone simply by pulling on the working end. Tied in an attractive cord or string in a contrasting colour to the package, this lashing, with its pleasant zigzag effect, can be used to gift-wrap boxes and cartons, even though they may be sufficiently secure without the lashing.

1 Tie a small fixed loop in one end of the line; then pull a bight from the standing part up through it.

2 Lead the standing end away from the bight, around and up behind the object being parcelled.

3 Pull a second bight from the standing part down through the first bight already made.

4 Lead the standing end away from the second bight, around and down behind the parcel; then pull a third bight from the standing part, up through the second bight.

5 Repeat steps 2 and 3, pulling a fourth bight down through the third bight.

6 Continue with interlacing alternate bights until the end of the parcel is reached; pull the working end completely through the last bight.

7 Lead the working end once around the almost completed parcel, prior to tucking it beneath itself.

8 Finally, dog the working end around its own standing part to secure.

Ocean Plait

This good-looking design can be executed in the finest twines or the thickest ropes. Consequently it may be used as a table mat or coaster, an embellishment for bandsmen and women's uniforms, a doormat, or you might frame one and hang it on the wall.

Pin thicker materials on to a cork board or polystyrene tile to keep them in place until you have made the final locking tuck.

1 Cast an anticlockwise (counter-clockwise) overhand loop in it with one end of a fairly long length of line.

2 Bend the long working end around (to the left) and lay it over the standing end of the original loop.

3 Take the end up and lay it (from left to right) over the top loop.

4 Lead the working end diagonally down (from right to left) and lay it on top of the lower loop.

5 Pick up the other half of the line – which now becomes the working end – and lay it (from left to right) over the new standing part.

6 Tuck the end diagonally (up and to the right), under/under, through the nearest loop.

7 Bring the working end around and take it diagonally from right to left over/under/over/under the knot parts.

8 Tuck the working end diagonally again (this time up from left to right), going over/under/over/under/over so that it comes out at the bottom right.

9 Tuck the working end up alongside the standing part, following the original lead around to double or triple the knot.

Six-Strand Round Plait

Create strong, flexible ropes with this process, using strands of different colours to discover the various possible patterns. Making this braid will be difficult at first – but it is well worth persisting for the striking end-product. Having said that, children can enjoy the various patterns that emerge when different coloured strands are used to make this plait.

1 Seize six strands, three of one colour alternately spaced between three of another (or, if all are of one colour, then mark the end of every other one with a felt-tipped pen).

2 Turn each yellow strand – in this example – down anticlockwise (counterclockwise), over the adjacent red strand.

3 Lift up the red strands and pull down evenly on each yellow strand in turn.

4 Turn one of the red strands down (clockwise) over the top of its adjacent yellow strand.

5 Lift the yellow strand up to contain and hold the turned-down red one.

6 Turn another red strand down (clockwise) over the top of its adjacent yellow strand.

7 Lift the yellow strand up to contain and hold this second turned-down red one.

8 Turn the remaining red strand down over the top of the last of the yellow strands.

9 Lift the third of the yellow strands up to join the other two.

10 Repeat this trio of paired movements – one strand going down, the other coming up – until the desired length of plait (braid) is achieved.

Glossary

ABSEIL A climber's self-controlled descent of an anchored – and often retrievable – climbing rope.

ANCHORAGE Boating – a general term that refers to moorings and the bending of cordage (by means of hitches) to various attachments; climbing – a safe belaying point.

ARAMIDES The first commercial manmade (synthetic) fibres do not melt when heated. Their high cost limits them to specialized applications.

BARREL KNOT see Blood Knot.

BELAY Boating – to make fast to a cleat or pin, often with a round turn followed by a figure-of-eight (or two) and then another round turn; climbing – the method of securing a climber in case of a fall.

BEND A name given to any one of the knots that bind (bend) two separate ropes together.

BIGHT A slack part of rope or other cordage between the two ends, particularly when it forms a partial loop.

BLOOD KNOT Any one of the strong and secure knots that depend upon numerous wrapping turns, favoured by anglers, cavers and climbers. (The name is derived from a limited surgical use.)

BRAID A term generally interchangeable with plait; but one that is sometimes stated to refer only to strands interwoven to make a flat pattern. (See also Plait.)

BREAKING STRENGTH The manufacturer's estimation of the load a rope will bear before it ruptures, expressed in kilograms and tonnes, taking no account of wear and tear, shock loading or knots that may reduce the figure drastically. (See also Safe Working Load.)

CABLE Strictly speaking, three righthanded hawsers (laid up lefthanded) make a nine-strand cable; but the term may also be loosely applied to any large length of rope.

CAPSIZE What occurs when a knot layout is distorted due to overloading, misuse or careless tightening. It may also be done deliberately as a means of quick release.

CARABINER See Karabiner.

CORD Small stuff under 10 mm/$^5/_{12}$ in diameter.

CORE Fibres, yarns and laid or braided materials that inertly fill the unwanted space at the heart of a four (or more) strand rope, or that actively contribute desirable qualities, such as strength or elasticity to sheath-and-core ropes.

DOG To improvise a temporary running eye by making a bight in the working end of cord, around its own standing part, and then tucking the end several times to trap it in place.

EFFICIENCY The actual strength of a knot in a rope or cord, expressed as a percentage of its theoretical breaking strength.

ELBOW Two crossing points created by an extra twist in a loop.

EYE A small round loop.

FIBRE The smallest element in all vegetable rope and cordage.

FILAMENT See Monofilament.

FRAY The accidental or deliberate unlaying of a rope's end to its component strands, yarns and fibres, multi- or monofilaments.

HARD LAID Stiff cordage.

HAWSER Any three-strand rope.

HEART See Core.

HITCH Any knot used to make a line fast to an anchorage such as a rail, spar, post, ring or another rope.

KARABINER A D-shaped or pear-shaped metal snap-ring, with a pivoting gate that can be securely closed, used by cavers and climbers.

KERNMANTEL Climbing rope construction consisting of a core (or kern), often of parallel bunches of fibres contained within a tightly woven protective sheath.

KINK A damaging deformation caused by an over-tight loop.

KNOT The term for stoppers, loops and self-sufficient bindings (thus excluding bends or hitches); also the generic word for all rope and cordage tucks and ties.

LANYARD A short length of cord that is used to lash, secure or suspend an object.

LAY The direction in which rope strands spiral as they go away from from the viewer, either clockwise (righthanded, Z-laid) or anticlockwise/counterclockwise (lefthanded, S-laid).

LEAD (Pronounced "leed") The direction taken by the working end as it goes around or through an object or knot.

LINE Any rope with a specific function (for example, a tow line or washing line).

LOCKING TUCK The concluding lead of a working end that secures any knot in its finished form, without which it would unravel or collapse.

LOOP A bight with a crossing point.

MAKE FAST To attach a line to an anchorage or belay (often with a hitch).

MESSENGER The name for a throwing or heaving line when it is used to pull a thicker cord or rope across an intervening space.

MIDDLE Used as a verb, to double a rope or cord so as to locate its centre.

MONOFILAMENT Continuous synthetic fibre of uniform diameter and circular cross-section larger than 50 micons/$\frac{1}{500}$ in. (See also Multifilament.)

MULTIFILAMENT Very fine continuous synthetic fibre of uniform diameter and circular cross section less than 50 microns/$\frac{1}{500}$ in. (See also Monofilament.)

NATURAL FIBRE Processed plant products used to make rope and other cordage.

NIP The point within a knot where friction may be concentrated.

NOOSE A free-running, sliding or adjustable loop.

NYLON The first synthetic (manmade) fibre of merit available to the cordage industry. There are two grades: Nylon 66 is extensively used in the UK and USA; Nylon 6 (made available under trade names such as Perlon and Enkalon) is widely used in Europe and Japan, as well as being available in the UK and USA.

OVERHAND LOOP A loop (clockwise or anticlockwise/ counterclockwise) in which the working end is laid on top of the standing part. (See also Loop.)

PLAIT A term generally interchangeable with braid, but which can refer only to interwoven strands forming a pattern that is three-dimensional in cross-section. (See also Braid.)

POLYESTER A widely used synthetic cordage (trade names Dacron and Terylene).

POLYETHYLENE A polyolefin synthetic (manmade) fibre (commonly known as Polythene/plastic).

POLYPROPYLENE A versatile polyolefin synthetic fibre.

PRUSIKING To climb a rope using a knot that jams when downward pressure is applied but can slide up the rope when the weight is removed.

RAPPEL See Abseil.

REEF Boating – to reduce sail area in strong winds (verb); each individual fold or roll of sail taken in (noun).

ROPE Cordage over 10 mm/$\frac{5}{12}$ in in diameter.

ROUND TURN In which a working end completely encircles a ring, rail, post or rope, and finishes up alongside its own standing part. (See also Turn.)

S-LAID Lefthanded (anticlockwise/ counterclockwise).

SAFE WORKING LOAD The estimated load a rope may withstand, taking into account various weakening factors (wear and tear, damage, effect of knots and other uses); it may be as little as one-seventh the quoted breaking strength. (See Breaking Strength.)

SECURITY The integral stability of a knot.

SLING An endless rope or webbing (tape) band or strop.

SMALL STUFF A casual term for any cordage, not rope.

SOFT LAID Any flexible rope and cordage.

SPLIT FILM Synthetic (manmade), ribbon-like fibres produced from a plastic sheet.

STANDING END The inactive end of cord. (See also Working End.)

STANDING PART That part of a rope or cord anywhere between working and standing ends.

STAPLE FIBRES Graded natural fibres of limited length and strength, due to their plant origins; also discontinuous synthetic (manmade) fibres created by cutting filaments into discrete lengths.

STRAND The largest element of a rope, made from contra-twisted yarns.

STRENGTH The integral ability of knotted cordage to withstand a load.

STRING Relatively cheap and disposable small cord and twine.

STROP See Sling.

SYNTHETIC ROPE Cordage that is made from synthetic (manmade) multifilaments, monofilaments, staple fibres or split film.

TAG END Angling – working end.

THIMBLE A metal or plastic lining for an eye.

THREAD Fine line.

TURN A 360 degree wrap around a rig, rail, post or rope. (See also Round Turn.)

UNDERHAND LOOP A loop in which the working end is laid beneath the standing part.

WHIPPING A binding to prevent a rope's end from fraying.

WORKING END The active end of a rope or cord. (See also Standing End.)

YARN The basic element of rope strands, spun from natural fibres or synthetic (manmade) materials.

Z-LAID Righthanded (clockwise).

A

Albright special, 44-5
alpine butterfly bend, 51
angler's loop, 92
Asher's equalizer, 84

B

Bachmann knot, 66
bends, 38-61
Bimini twist, 101
bindings, 80-103
blood knot, 40-41
blood loop dropper knot, 96
boa knot, 82-3
boom hitch, 56-7
bottle sling, 86-7
bowline, Brummycham, 97
braided ropes, 18
breaking strengths, 20-1
Brummycham bowline, 97
button knots, Chinese, 78-9

C

caver's helical knot, 69
chain, simple, 116-17
chain stitch lashing, 118-19
Chi-Fi knot, 75
Chinese button knots, 78-9
Chinese lanyard knot, 76-7
climbing ropes, 19
clinging Clara, 54
clove hitch, 27
coils, 22-3
common thief knot, 50
cross-prusik knot, 70
cutting ends, 25

D

diamond hitch, 114-15

double fisherman's knot, 35
double ring hitching, 112
drawloop, overhand knot
    with, 30
dropper knot, blood loop, 96

E

ends, cutting and securing, 25

F

fids, 24
figure-of-eight: double, 95
  triple, 100
figure-of-eight hitch, double, 85
fireman's chair knot, 102-3
fisherman's knots, 35
French Prusik knot, extended, 74
Frost knots, 93-4

G

Gordian knot, 10-11
gripfids, 24

H

hangman's noose, 98-9
heat sealing ends, 25
Heddon knots, 70-1
hemp rope, 15, 16

highwayman's hitch, 53
history, 8-13
hitches, 38-61
hitching: double ring, 112
  ringbolt, 110

I

icicle hitch, 58
inspecting ropes, 22-3

J

Jansik special, 61
jar sling, 86-7
jug sling, 86-7
jury mast knot, 106

K

Klemheist knot, 67
knots, 62-79
kreuzklem, 70

L

laid ropes, 18
lanyard knots, Chinese, 76-7
"law of hitch and bight", 27
lighterman's hitch, 59
loops, 80-103

plaited ropes, 19
pliers, round-billed, 24
Poldo tackle, 107
Prusik knots, 64-5
  extended French, 74

R
racking bend, 42
release hitches, 72-3
ringbolt hitching, 110
ropes: breaking strengths, 20-1
  care of, 22-3
  history, 8-13
  materials, 14-17
  strength and security, 34
  terminology, 26-7
  types of, 18-19

S
scaffold knots, 37
security, 34
seizing bend, 43
shake hands, 49
sheath-and-core ropes, 19
simple chains, 116-17
simple knot, 30
simple Simon double, 48
simple Simon over, 46
simple Simon under, 47
sisal rope, 15
sliding loop, 33
spade end knot, 91

M
mariner's knot, 68
materials, 14-17
monkey's fist, 108-9

N
natural fibres, 14-16
needles, netting, 24
noose, hangman's, 98-9
nylon rope, 16, 17

O
ocean plait, 120-1
ossel hitch, 55
overhand knots, 30
  double, 31
  triple, 32
  two strand, 31
  with drawloop, 30

P
Palomar knot, 60
Penberthy knot, 69
plafond knot, 76
plaits: six-strand round, 122-3
  eight-strand square, 113

square Turk's head, 88-9
strangle knot, 32
strength, 34
surgeon's loop, 33
Swedish fids, 24
synthetic cordage, 16-17, 18

T
taping ends, 25
terminology, 26-7
thumb knot, 30
tools, 24
true lover's knot, 13,
tumbling thief knot, 50
Turk's heads: square, 88-9
  twined, 90

V
vegetable fibre cordage, 14-16, 18
versatackle, 111
vibration-proof hitch, 52

W
whipping, perfected, 36
wire loops, 24

Further Information

SUPPLIERS

English Braids, Spring Lane, Malvern WR14 1AL
Tel: 01684 892 222
Fax: 01684 892 111
Their marine sales division caters for the recreational sector and sail boat racing. Suppliers of barrier ropes, starter cords, shock cords, whipping twines, webbing and web-lash securing systems, and stainless steel hollow fids. Contact them for the location of your nearest stockist.

Eurorope Limited, 4 Phoenix Court, Atkinson Way, Foxhills Industrial Estate, Scunthorpe DN15 8QJ
Tel: 01724 280 480
Fax: 01724 857 750
Wholesale suppliers of rope, cord, twines, nets, lifting gear slings and accessories. Contact them for the location of your nearest stockist.

Des & Liz Pawson, Footrope Knots, 501 Wherstead Road, Ipswich, Suffolk IP2 8LL
Tel: 01473 690 090
Suppliers of traditional rope, cordage and smaller stuff; wire rope and chain; canvas; tools; fittings; fenders, knotboards, chest beckets and other knotwork; books (new, secondhand and rare). Their unique ropework museum may be visited free (by prior arrangement).

Kevin Keatley, K.J.K. Ropeworks, Town Living Farmhouse, Puddington, Tiverton, Devon EX16 8LW
Tel/fax: 01884 860 692
Supplier of cords and fittings, especially braided synthetics. Price list on request.

Leanda, 39 Borrowdale Drive, Norwich, Norfolk NR1 4LY
Tel/fax: 01603 434 707
Textile craft equipment manufacturers; specialists in Japanese-style braiding and passementerie equipment; accessories for spinning and weaving; also a book list.

Marlow Ropes Ltd, Diplocks Way, Hailsham, East Sussex BN27 3JS
Tel: 01323 847 234
Fax: 01323 440 093
email: yachting@marlow ropes.com
Website: http://www.marlow ropes.com
Market leaders in yacht rope technology and such accessories as shockcord, barrier ropes, toestrap and buoyancy bag webbing, whipping twine, splicing kits, sail repair tapes.

Ann Norman, Sagaman, Aston Road, Bampton, Oxfordshire, OX18 2AL
Tel/fax: 01993 850 823
email: sagaman@compuserve.com
Designer, handweaver and maker of cords, including four-strand cords, and ropes of traditional laid structure. Advice offered and commissions accepted.

Oakhurst Quality Products Limited, Warsop Trading Estate, Hever Road, Edenbridge, Kent TN8 5LD
Tel: 01732 866 668
Fax: 01732 864 555
Wholesale suppliers of rope, twine, cordage, chain, doormats, work gloves, garden sundries. Contact Brenda Risdon for the location of your nearest stockist.

BIBLIOGRAPHY

Asher, Harry, *The Alternative Knot Book* (Nautical Books, A. & C. Black, London, 1989)
Ashley, Clifford Warren, *The Book of Knots* (Doubleday, New York, 1944/Faber & Faber, London, 1947)
Bailey, Hazel, *Knotting for Guides* (Girl Guides Association, London, 1987)
Chisnall, Robert (Editor), *Rock Climbing Safety Manual* (Ontario Rock Climbing Association, Canada, 1984)
Day, Cyrus Lawrence, *Quipus & Witches' Knots* (University of Kansas Press, 1967)
Graumont, Raoul, and Hensel, John, *The Encyclopaedia of Knots and Fancy Rope Work* (Cornell Maritime Press, Cambridge, Maryland, 1939)
Graves, Richard H., *The Bushcraft Handbooks* (Graves, Sydney, 1952)
Griend, P. van de, and Turner, J.C. (eds), *The History and Science of Knots* (World Scientific Publishing Company, Singapore, New Jersey, London, Hong Kong, 1996)
I.G.K.T., *Knotting Matters* (1982 to the present)
Kreh, Lefty, and Sosin, Mark, *Practical Fishing & Boating Knots* (A. & C. Black, London, 1975)
Luebben, Craig, *Knots for Climbers* (Chockstone Press, Evergreen, Colorado, 1993)
March, Bill, *Mountain Rope Techniques* (Cicerone Press, Cumbria, 1983)
Noonan, Michael, *Climbing Knots – for Lefties and Righties* (I.C.S. Books, Merryville, Indiana, 1997)
Padgett, Allen, & Smith, Bruce, *On Rope* (National Speliological Society, Huntsville, Alabama, 1992)
Payne, Lee and Bob, "The Forgotten Zeppelin Knot" (*Boating Magazine*, March 1976)
Perkins, Andy, Tapes, *Slings & Harnesses* (Troll Safety Equipment, 1991)
Rosenow, Frank, *Seagoing Knots* (W.W. Norton, New York, 1990)
Shaw, George Russell, *Knots – Useful & Ornamental* (Bonanza Books, New York, 1924 and 1933)
Spencer, Charles L., *Knots, Splices & Fancy Work* (Brown, Son & Fergusson, Glasgow, 1934)
Sweet, John, *Scout Pioneering* (Scout Association, London, 1974)
Toss, Brion, *The Rigger's Apprentice* International Marine Publishing Co, Camden, Maine, 1984)
Trower, Nola, *Knots and Ropework* (Helmsman Books, Marlborough, Wiltshire, 1992)
Vare, Alan B., *The Hardy Book of Fisherman's Knots* (Camden Publishing, London, 1987)
Warner, Charles, *A Fresh Approach to Knotting and Ropework* (Warner, Yanderra, NSW, 1992)

ACKNOWLEDGEMENTS

The author is indebted to David Ierston, marine sales manager for English Braids Ltd, who supplied superb cordage for this book.

The following, from whom the cordage was obtained to tie most of the specimen knots illustrated, were also generous with their time and advice: Brenda Risdon (Oakhurst Quality Products Ltd.); Kevin Keatley (K.J.K. Ropeworks); James Martin (Marlow Ropes Ltd.); Des & Liz Pawson (Footrope Knots).

A special extra acknowledgement is due to Des Pawson who, by allowing access to his home and workplace, made possible the unique portraits of traditional ropework that enrich this book.

ORGANIZATIONS

The International Guild of Knot Tyers was established in 1982 and now has a worldwide membership. It is a registered educational charity, dedicated to preserving and promoting the art, craft and science of knots.

Anyone – expert or novice – interested in tying knots may join. IGKT members enjoy a quarterly magazine, *Knotting Matters*, in addition to regular meetings. For more details and an application form, contact:

Nigel Harding,
IGKT Honorary Secretary,
16 Egles Grove, Uckfield, East Sussex TN22 2BY, England
Tel: 01825 760 425
e-mail: igkt@nigelharding.demon.uk
(Knotting can also be found on the Internet.)